BOOKS FOR FAMILY READING,

Published by D. Appleton & Company.

MRS. ELLIS'S NEW WORKS.

I.

SOCIAL DISTINCTIONS; OR, HEARTS AND HOMES.

By MRS. ELLIS, Author of "The Women of England," &c.

'This work should find a place in every family; it is one of the best productions of this excellent writer, full of deep and touching interest, and urging lessons of great practical importance."

II.

PREVENTION BETTER THAN CURE;

OR THE MORAL WANTS OF THE WORLD WE LIVE IN.

By MRS. ELLIS. 1 vol. 12mo. Price 50 cts. paper cover, 75 cts. cloth.

"We can safely recommend the book to mothers and daughters who would prize useful hints on the conduct of life, and practical directions for self-management."—*Christian Enquirer*

MISS M'INTOSH'S WORKS.

I.

CHARMS AND COUNTER-CHARMS.

By MARIA J. M'INTOSH, Author of "Conquest and Self Conquest," "Praise and Principle," &c. Complete in one handsome volume, 12mo., cloth $1; or in two parts, paper, 75 cts.

This work will be found one of the most impressive and beautiful tales of the day. The moral is felicitously developed, and is true in thought and feeling.

II.

TWO LIVES; OR, TO SEEM AND TO BE.

By MARIA J. M'INTOSH. 1 vol. 12mo., paper cover 50 cts., cloth 75 cts.

"The previous works of Miss M'Intosh, although issued anonymously, have been popular in the best sense of the word. The simple beauty of her narratives, combining pure sentiment with high principle, and noble views of life and its duties, ought to win for them a hearing at every fireside in our land. We have rarely perused a tale more interesting and instructive than the one before us, and we commend it most cordially to the attention of all our readers."—*Prot. Churchman.*

III.

AUNT KITTY'S TALES.

By MARIA J. M'INTOSH. A new edition, complete in one vol., 12mo., cloth 75 cts.

This volume contains the following interesting stories: "Blind Alice," "Jessie Graham," "Florence Arnott," "Grace and Clara," "Ellen Leslie, or The Reward of Self-Control."

MISS SEWELL'S WORKS.

I.

MARGARET PERCIVAL: A TALE.

Edited by the Rev. WM. SEWELL, B. A 2 vols., 12mo., paper cover $1, cloth $1 50

II.

GERTRUDE: A TALE.

Edited by the Rev. WM. SEWELL, B. A 12mo., cloth 75 cts, paper cover 50 cts.

III.

AMY HERBERT: A TALE.

Edited by the Rev. WM. SEWELL, B. A. 1 vol. 12mo., cloth 75 cts., paper cover 50 cts.

IV.

LANETON PARSONAGE: A TALE.

Edited by the Rev. WM. SEWELL, B. A. 3 vols. 12mo., cloth $2 25 paper cover $1 50.

WOMAN IN AMERICA.

WOMAN IN AMERICA:

HER WORK AND HER REWARD.

BY

MARIA J. McINTOSH,

AUTHOR OF "CHARMS AND COUNTER-CHARMS," "TO SEEM AND TO BE," ETC. ETC.

"The ancients looked towards the land of the setting sun as to a land of promise, where the earth puts forth fruits for eternal life; and surely the home of the Hesperides must have features and beauty of its own, and a calling not known to the old world."

F. BREMER.

NEW YORK:

D. APPLETON & COMPANY, 200 BROADWAY.

PHILADELPHIA:

GEO. S. APPLETON, 164 CHESNUT-STREET.

M DCCC L.

CONTENTS.

INTRODUCTION.

HE who undertakes to mark the movements of a multitude, who would decide whither their steps tend, and judge their deviations from the right path, must stand above them, that he may overlook their course; and some such elevation may seem to be claimed by her who seeks to awaken the attention of her countrywomen to the mistakes by which, as she believes, their social progress is impeded, or misdirected. The only advantage over those whom she addresses claimed by the author of the following pages, however, is opportunity for more extended observation of the varied forms of social life in her own land, than has been enjoyed by many of her sex.

Bound to the South—the land of her birth, and the home of her childhood and youth—by ties which no time can sever, ties knit when feeling was strongest and association most vivid, her maturer and more reflective years have been passed in the Northern States; and here kind hearts have been opened to her, and friendly hands have been extended to draw her into the sanctuary of their homes, and permit her to become a pleased witness of the "holy revealings" proceeding from those innermost shrines of life. Nor has her observation been confined to one class, in these her different abodes. She has been permitted to take her views of life, now from the position occupied by those who claim the "*privilege*" of idleness, and now from that of those whom a friendly necessity has constrained to yield obedience to the benign law of labor.

Thus, her sympathies with all have been cultivated; and if somewhat of dogmatism be discoverable in this little volume, it will, she hopes, be pardoned in one who can say—"We speak that we know, and testify that we have seen."

NEW YORK, *Jan.* 18*th*, 1850.

WOMAN IN AMERICA:

HER WORK AND HER REWARD.

CHAPTER I.

NATURAL PRINCIPLES, AND THEIR APPLICATION TO MORAL SUBJECTS.

He who acknowledges God in the creation of our earth, can need no labored argument to prove that He preserves it in being, and rules over its destinies. Were all things around us fixed and changeless in their character, we might be in danger of forgetting, or overlooking the present Deity; but our existence passes amidst ever varying scenes. Death and Life are unceasingly busy around us—the one resolving all things into their original elements, the other evoking from those elements new forms of grace and beauty. Each Spring, the Spirit of God moves over the face of the dead earth, quickens it into new life, decks it with primeval beauty, and awakens, from the silence in which stern winter had bound them, all the sweet harmonies of nature—the ripple of the brook—the dash of the wave—the low hum of the bee—the cheerful chirp of the insect—"the charm of earliest birds,"

> "That, singing, up to Heaven-gate ascend,"

and those "vernal airs" which,

> "Breathing the smell of field and grove, attune
> "The trembling leaves."

To the freshness of spring succeeds the luxuriance of Summer, and the maturer loveliness of Autumn, whose first gorgeous coloring,

> "The gilded halo hovering round decay,"

fades, even as we gaze, into soberer hues, preparing us for the last great change effected by Winter, which by its first icy touch hushes the bounding pulse of life in "Nature's full, free heart," and stripping the earth of all her bright array, wraps her in a snowy shroud, and leaves her to rest in the solemn beauty of the grave.

Thus are we ever reminded in the natural world of the presence of the creating and guiding Spirit; and if, in the moral world, that presence is, from the nature of things, less obvious to the senses, are not the arguments for it more conclusive to the reason? Are not sentient and intelligent beings of more value than the fairest forms which no spirit animates? Can the Infinitely Wise thus paint the flower, provide for the thirsting earth all the soft influences of sun and shower, kindle the lights that give glory to the solemn night, and deck the blue arch of heaven with the light gauzy clouds that veil the mid-day sun, or the gorgeous drapery of gold and crimson behind which he sinks to rest;—shall He furnish the lower orders of the animal creation with an unerring guide whereby they may secure to themselves the highest good of which they are capable, and avoid all those evils that threaten their brief existence;—and shall man, the being created in His own image, gifted with senses the most acute and intellect the most far-reaching, with a physical organization through which he has become heir to a thousand ills, and a spirit whose longings are foreshadowings of that immortality for which a Divine revelation has declared him destined—shall he be nature's only orphan, finding in the Universal Father but a conscientious Ruler, who, having arranged the mechanism of His government on just and sound principles, leaves him, with unpitying eye and unhelping hand, to work out his destiny for time and for eternity? Not thus did He teach who questioned, "Shall He so clothe the grass of the field, which to-day is and to-morrow is cast into the oven, and shall He not much more clothe you, O ye of little faith ?"

This is a subject on which we believe there is more inconsideration that needs to be aroused to thought, and more insensibility that requires to be quickened into feeling, than infidelity to be convinced. We have therefore rather sought to present a vivid picture of the truth, than to construct an argument for its defence. But if it be admitted that the Great Spirit who presides over the natural phenomena of our world, arranges also its moral and social influences, will it not follow that those principles which are invariably manifested in the one will reappear in the other? If it be acknowledged that man, with his powers of thought and feeling and action, with his ever-extending capacities and limitless desires, is not less cared for by Him than the lily of the field which He clothes with such delicate beauty, or the bird which He sustains in the air, may we not believe that at least equal excellence of design and carefulness of adjustment will be discoverable to an earnestly attentive eye in those arrangements of His Providence by which the character and the destiny of the one are so greatly influenced, as in those which give its charm to the brief existence of the other?

Now let us glance at some of those principles which are most frequently discoverable in the natural world. The first of these that presents itself to our observation is, that nothing is created in vain—that from the sun, which is the most glorious natural type of Him whose smile is

> "the life and light
> Of all this wondrous world we see,"

to the smallest animalcule that sports in its beams, undetected save by the aid of the most powerful microscope, each has been created for a specific object, for the accomplishment of which it is carefully fitted. So far as our limited faculties permit us to appreciate the facts of nature, existence is pleasurable to each creature, yet none seems to have been created only to enjoy. In his remarks on Dr. Mantell's interesting work on animalcules, Chambers says: "Nor is *this* a study the result of which is merely amusement and wonder; for, like the minute parasitic vegetation whose growth absorbs the elements of decay, and which occasionally create such havoc among human food and engender disease and death, the myriad animalcules in nature may execute similar missions, sometimes repressing putridity, at others becoming the sources of the most loathsome and fatal diseases."

And if these are not exempt from their tasks—if they have an appointed office to fulfil in the laboratory of the universe, can creatures more nobly endowed be intended only as idle consumers of the gifts of God?

Another principle, which has been so often demonstrated that we are scarcely permitted to doubt its universality, is, that in those objects which seem to the superficial eye formed but to charm, and to give, by their beauty and their grace, dim intimations of fairer and brighter scenes, there dwells some ulterior power, rendering them useful as well as ornamental. He who goes forth at the soft hour "when daylight dies," and watches the bright stars, as they come out one by one in the deep serene of night, may well exclaim—"How beautiful!" But is this all? Can any one now believe that these were created but to adorn this fair abode of man? Has not science revealed to us in them floods of being, before the mighty imagination of which our weak minds sink appalled? The clouds which float so gracefully across the blue vault of heaven, "deck the gorgeous west at even" with colors that defy the painter's art, or, gathering in stormy grandeur around the mountain's head, add new sublimity to nature, bear in their bosom the fertilizing shower. And even in the flower which rears its graceful head in our path, and sheds its perfume on the air we breathe, we are often taught to recognise, and may always suspect, higher uses than these.

A third principle in the arrangements of the natural world, and the last which we shall at present notice, is that beautiful system of adaptation by which each object in creation finds itself in that position for which its peculiar organization has fitted it, and discovers in its offices the exact correlatives of its powers.

From the application of these natural principles to the moral world, it will follow, first, that every distinct class of moral and intellectual beings should have—that is, was designed to have—a specific object in the exercise of its powers, in its moral and intellectual life, apart from the pleasure of that exercise; secondly, that with none can this object be merely to give a new charm to the existence of others, to add beauty to the scenes of which they make a part,—that this is, in truth, only a necessary and unconscious result of their faithful performance of their true and allotted work; and, lastly, that this work will bear such a relation to the powers and position of the actors, that it may be easily and certainly deduced from them.

It is the object of the present work, as its title purports, to refer these principles to the life of woman, and especially to determine from her position in America, and her powers, as developed by that position, what is the work designed for her here, and what the reward which awaits its performance.

CHAPTER II.

WOMAN—HER OFFICES AND HER POWERS.

How many eloquent theses have been written, and how much logic wasted, to prove the equality of the sexes! It seems to us, that the writers and speakers on this subject would have done well to commence by defining their terms. What is meant by equality as here used? Is it intended to convey the idea that the soul of woman is as precious to the Father of Spirits as that of man; that woman has an equal interest with man in all those great events which have marked the dealings of God with His intelligent creation on our earth, from the hour in which Adam, awaking from a deep sleep, found beside him the companion of his sinless and happy life, to the present moment, when the sin-stricken and sorrowing soul of man, echoing the divine conviction that it is not good for him to be alone, still seeks in woman his "help-meet" in the labors, the trials, and sufferings of mortality? Are we to understand from it that woman, equally with man, has a trust committed to her by the Judge of all, for the fulfilment of which she will be held responsible? Can these things be matters of doubt? Were not Mary and Martha loved as well as Lazarus? Did not the soul of Anna kindle with as divine an inspiration as that of Simeon, when she held in her arms the infant Saviour?

Or is the question, whether woman exerts an equally important influence over the character and destinies of our race? This can scarcely be a question to one familiar with the records of Paradise and of Bethlehem.

And yet the unqualified assertion of equality between the sexes, would be contradicted alike by sacred and profane history. There is a political inequality, ordained in Paradise, when God said to the woman, "He shall rule over thee," and which has ever existed, in every tribe, and nation, and people of earth's countless multitudes. Let those who would destroy this inequality, pause ere they attempt to abrogate a law which emanated from the all-perfect Mind. And let not woman murmur at the seeming lowliness of her lot. There is a dignity which wears no outward badge, an elevation recognised by no earthly homage. This wise, and for her most happy inequality, secludes woman from the arena of political contention, with its strifes and rivalries, its mean jealousies and meaner pretensions, in the quiet home where truth may show herself unveiled, and peace may dwell unmolested. She hears the thunders of no battle-field drowning the "still, small voice" of conscience echoing the divine command, "Thou shalt do no murder." All the influences of that lot to which God assigned her, are calculated to nurture in her that meek and lowly spirit with which He delights to dwell.

Subjected to influences so diverse, man and woman could scarcely have preserved entire identity in their spiritual natures, even had they been originally the same. But that they were so will seem doubtful, at least, to those who know how much spiritual manifestations—all we can know of spirit here—are dependent upon physical organization; and who, recognising the different spheres of action appointed to man and to woman, recall one of the general principles already advanced, viz. that each creature in the universe finds itself in that position for which its peculiar organization has fitted it, and discovers in its offices the exact correlatives of its powers.

Different offices and *different* powers—this is what we would assert of them, leaving to others the vain question of equality or inequality. Each seems to us equally important to the fulfilment of God's designs in the formation, the preservation, and the perfection of human society.

The stout heart and strong hand of man are obviously needed in every successive stage of social organization, from its earliest attempts to the highest development it has yet attained. There has been a time predicted, indeed, and we humbly hope there are already tokens that this good time is coming, when "the wolf shall dwell with the lamb, and the leopard shall lie down with the kid, and the young lion and the fatling together, and a little child shall lead them;" that is, when the passions which have made mankind like ferocious animals shall be subdued, and a little child—the type of love—shall lead those for whom bolts and bars had been needed. But till that period arrive, would not our earth be as one wide Bedlam were it not that the strong arm of government supplies outward restraints for those who have no restraining principle within? And this government—is it not clearly man's province? Has it not been committed to him by Heaven, and is not the nature with which he has been gifted the seal of that commission? Law is an uncompromising, inexorable power; can it be the product of a gentle woman's mind? It must be upheld by a force which will prove opposition bootless; does that belong to woman?

But while all the outward machinery of government, the body, the thews and sinews of society, are man's, woman, if true to her own not less important or less sacred mission, controls its vital principle. Unseen herself, working, like nature, in secret, she regulates its pulsations, and sends forth from its heart, in pure and temperate flow, the life-giving current. It is hers to warm into life the earliest germs of thought and feeling in the infant mind, to watch the first dawning of light upon the awakening soul, to aid the first faint struggles of the clay-encumbered spirit to grasp the beautiful realities which here and there present themselves amid the glittering falsities of earth, and to guide its first tottering steps into the paths of peace. And who does not feel how her warm affections and quick irrepressible sympathies fit her for these labors of love? As the young immortal advances in his career, he comes to need a severer discipline, and man, with his unconceding reason and stern resolve, becomes his teacher. Yet think not that woman's work is done when the child has passed into the youth, or the youth into the man. Still, as disease lays its hand heavily upon the strong frame, and sorrow wrings the proud heart of man, she, "the help-meet," if faithful to her allotted work, is at his side, teaching him to bend to the storms of life, that he may not be broken by them; humbly stooping herself, that she may remove from his path every "stone of stumbling," and gently leading him onward and upward to a Divine Consoler, with whose blessed ministerings the necessities of a more timid spirit and a feebler physical organization have made her familiar.

It may be thought that we have already penetrated to the heart of our subject, and exhausted all its capabilities; but we have, in truth, only touched its surface, giving the faintest outline of those distinctive characteristics which permit us to consider the work and the reward of woman, apart from that of man. Let it be remembered, that to every thing in nature there is a passive as well as an active aspect. Thus, while woman does much to form the nation, whose council-halls will bear the impress of those forms into which she has greatly aided to mould its homes, the nation, the laws, customs, and habits of the society in which she dwells, will do much to form her. It follows from this, that while the grand elements of character which distinguish woman as a class, are the same everywhere and at all times, the combination of these into the individual woman is almost infinitely varied. This is a necessary result of that often iterated principle, that the great Author of nature and Disposer of the circumstances of human life, never repeats Himself.

Go out into the forest when its summer foliage makes its recesses dim with shade; what arithmetic would suffice to number the leaves which dance with such glad life to the soft music of the south wind? As well might you attempt to number the stars of heaven, or the sands upon the seashore. And yet we doubt whether of all those countless myriads, two could be found so exactly alike that no difference of shape or shade should mark to a careful observer their individuality. Thus is it with the human face; for though we have heard of doubles among men, that is, of two men between whom there existed so perfect a resemblance that each might pass for the other, we suspect that could they be placed together, there would always be found some difference in the color of hair, or eyes, or complexion, some turn of countenance, some frown of the brow or smile of the lip, peculiar to one of them,—distinctions slight, it may be, yet sufficient to establish the personal identity of each. And thus, we believe, too, is it with the mental features.

We have not now, however, to do with those minute peculiarities stamping the individual character, but with those more widely extended, though less deeply marked traits which we term national. These are easily recognisable in the physical man. There are few who cannot distinguish at a glance the quick, mercurial Frenchman from the heavy, slow, but deep-thinking German, or the sturdy Englishman, less quick than the first, less profound than the last, yet, by his unwearied perseverance, accomplishing more than both put together. We believe that the peculiar social and political institutions of America must also produce a peculiar modification of character, in accordance with the law of adaptation already stated. Such a modification has indeed been already produced to a certain extent, but there have been counter-influences which have greatly limited this result. One of these counter-influences is to be found in the frequent and easy communication with other lands attainable in the present day; and another in that—shall we say national *humility?*—which makes us ever ready to yield our own sense of what is suitable, convenient, or agreeable, to the caprices of a leader of *ton* in London or Paris.

It is this last barrier to the perfect moral adaptation

of American women to American society, against which whatever influence this little book may claim will be exerted. We would, if possible, persuade American women to look at those points in their own condition which distinguish them from their sex elsewhere, and from this their favorable position, and from the power it confers on them, to augur what an important work has been committed to them, and what a noble destiny awaits them if thev are true to that work.

CHAPTER III.

GOD IN HISTORY—THE AMERICAN PEOPLE.

It may be well, perhaps, before taking another step in our argument, to pass rapidly over those by which we have arrived at our present position. The first assertion which we made and which we deemed no argument necessary to sustain, was that the Creator was likewise the Governor of our world, and therefore that we might expect to find the great principles of the natural world reasserted in the moral. On a survey of these principles, we found that nothing was created simply for its own enjoyment—that every creature had a work to do in the great laboratory of the universe, and that for its own peculiar work each was specially adapted by its organization.

From these *natural* principles we inferred that each class of *moral* and *intellectual* beings had also its appointed task, and that the task thus allotted to man and woman differed just in proportion to the different physical organization and spiritual *development,* at least, received from their Creator and moral Governor.

Another glance at the natural world showed us another fact; viz. that the great Author of nature never repeats Himself, but that leaf differs from leaf, and man from man. Let us dwell for a moment on this fact, and see how it harmonizes with the laws already announced. Each, it has been said, has his appropriate work to do, and in that work finds the exact correlative of his power, which power is the sum of his natural capabilities and of the circumstances in which he has been placed, and through which those capabilities must be developed and exercised. Now, is it not manifest that from the multiplied combinations resulting from the diversity of capabilities and of circumstances, we have the source of a variety in character and office limited only by the number of the earth's inhabitants?

But the laws of the great Ruler apply no less to national than to individual existences. He sent confusion among the Heaven-defying builders of Babel, that, driven asunder, they might people remote portions of the globe, and growing into nations under widely-differing influences, each might be moulded into that form necessary to render it the agent of His providence for special ends.

It would be interesting, indeed, holding in our hands the clue furnished by this principle of the adaptation of each existence, whether individual or national, to its appropriate work, to tread the inmost recesses of the labyrinth of history,—gathering in our passage new proofs of the goodness and wisdom of Him who ruleth over the inhabitants of earth, new cause for the humble prostration of our spirits before the King of kings and Lord of lords. There we should mark how amid the sombre despotism and the monster worship of Egypt had arisen a class of men, whose active minds desiring some avenue to power from which that despotism could not debar them, had sought and found it at the altar of the veiled Isis, Nature, whose secrets were typified by mystic rites and guarded in subterranean temples. We should see the science thus acquired wrought into more graceful forms by the polished Greeks, and under the comparative freedom of their institutions we should find the human mind trained to the discussion of all those great questions affecting its origin, its progress, and its destiny; and by that very discussion the depth of its darkness and the necessity of a Divine Teacher would be revealed to us. The results thus obtained we should find disseminated over the world by the indomitable power and boundless ambition of the haughty Roman, and the way thus prepared for the coming of Him who should be a "Light to lighten the Gentiles" as well as "the salvation of His people Israel." And in this people Israel we should discover the most indubitable proofs of Providential arrangement,—sequestered, as they were, from all other nations, their race preserved uncorrupted amid the extremes of proud elevation and of defeat, captivity, and exile, that the Messiah for whom they waited, only that they might reject him, should appear to all as indeed the promised Deliverer, He whom their prophets had predicted, and the antetypes of their history and their worship had alike foreshadowed.

So far, it is probable, most Christian readers of history have pursued the train of thought designated. But shall we pause here? Were the purposes of God towards our race accomplished with the coming of the Deliverer? Had they been, why delay the last act of the sublime drama—the end of all things?

Let us advance, still holding that clue which has guided us in safety so far. A few centuries pass away, during which, aided by the consolidation into one vast empire of almost the whole known world, and by the community of language and facility of intercourse thus produced, the Christian faith has extended itself nominally to nearly all the nations and tribes of men. Wherever the Roman standard floats, the cross—the symbol of sinning, suffering, and regenerated humanity—has met the eye, aroused the mind, and stirred the heart of man. But that symbol has become the badge of an earthly domination. The Church, grown proud in her prosperity, thinks no more of "fulfilling in her own body the measure of her Lord's sufferings,"—of devoting herself to the object for which He lived and died—the salvation of mankind. The removal to Byzantium of the imperial throne had left to the visible head of the Church, the Bishop of Rome, the supreme temporal authority over the Western nations. But that body, which was the keeper of the sacred archives whence man draws the law of his life and the charter of his immortality, could not be suffered to merge its nobler office in an earthly sovereignty, and Rome finally succumbed beneath the repeated attacks of those barbarian hordes led by the "Scourge of God" upon the sunny plains of Italy from the sounding shores of the Baltic, and the recesses of forests dark with the shade of ages. And here we see how, through the "darkest woof" of national as well as of individual life, "there runs the golden thread of love." The Church was driven back to her own proper sphere; she no longer wielded the sword of temporal power, but as the vicegerent of God, the medium through which His will was made known to the waiting spirit, she exercised soon a far higher sovereignty. The barbarian conqueror bowed at her footstool, levied tribute for her support, and led his armies in her defence. Whatever we may think of the Church of Rome at the present time, it is impossible not to recognise in her pompous ritual and gorgeous decoration, means admirably adapted to secure the homage of the untutored minds thus subjected to her influence; while in her uncompromising assertion of despotic authority in all matters of belief, we see the *only* power, humanly speaking, by which, through long ages of darkness, among fierce strifes and ever-changing political organizations, the true Christian faith, from which, amid all her perversions in practice, this church never long varied in principle, could have been preserved.

Christianity having once taken root in the earth, and having, nominally at least, extended its empire over those nations which were to be the earth's rulers, the great object for which Rome had been permitted to establish so wide a sovereignty was answered, and that sovereignty was broken up into many smaller states, in which variety of laws and social institutions produced variety of character. Still, however, over these states the Church maintained her spiritual supremacy. The fierce spirits of their barbarian inhabitants were thus tamed into reverence, and those who might have defied the Invisible were subdued into lowly submission before the visible representative of His power.

But the Church, becoming more and more corrupt in practice, less and less true to the faith she taught, at length betrayed so far her sacred mission as to make a traffic of the spiritual mysteries she held, that she might build up thereby her temporal magnificence. In doing this she proved that these mysteries, for the teaching of which she had been expressly organized, were to her but cunningly devised fables. The glory had departed from her, and had not the sceptre been wrested from her hands, the shadow of a universal skepticism would soon have fallen on our race. In the mean time, among the forests and hills of Germany, a people of thoughtful mind and earnest faith and courageous nature, had been preparing, from whom first arose the cry for the bread of life, in which all the northern nations of Europe soon joined. Macaulay, with that masterly vigor which ever marks his touch, has depicted the extent of the Reformation, and the political causes why it went so far and why it failed to go farther. May a humbler hand be permitted to add to these political causes, one which is the result of faith in that

—"Divinity which shapes our ends,
Rough-hew them how we will——"

These northern nations were not of higher intelligence or deeper piety than those who dwelt in warmer climes, but the stern contest with the unfriendly elements in which their lives were passed, and the character of their institutions, had given energy to their frames and independence to their spirits—had accustomed them to do their own thinking and their own fighting—had matured them into *men* who might now be trusted to defend the faith they had attained, from the attacks of infidelity on the one hand and of superstition on the other. The more southern nations of Europe, lulled in the lap of ease, their sky all sunshine and their earth all flowers, had become indolent and luxurious, and indolence and luxury had done its usual work upon them, enervating the mind as well as the body. Of little value to them would have been the right to judge for themselves. Elegant scholars, charming poets, exquisite artists were they, but thinking—thinking of so grave and stern a character as those subjects require which are involved in our religious faith—this was a labor which they would have preferred, probably, under any circumstances, to relinquish to others; and if they must be guided, better for them the Church of Rome, even with all the faults her worst enemies can attribute to her, than the reckless, mocking spirit of infidelity. To such minds, "to examine all things and hold fast that which is good," is a well-nigh impossible achievement—they believe all or reject all. Earnest and true believers were many of them in the church to which they committed themselves soul and body, and roused by her peril, they cast aside their luxury, forgot their sloth, and did battle for her valiantly with both sword and pen. She was still to them the representative of the Holy, and they could still worship through her "in spirit and in truth." Thus, through all the changes of the Reformation commenced by Luther, do we still see the Divine Wisdom presiding over the destinies of man—liberating from the thrall of superstition, not those who had attained to the highest civilization—who possessed the most acute and subtle intellects—but those nations, and those only, who, amidst an almost rude simplicity of life, had formed habits of earnest, truthful, and courageous thought, and whose strength, rough though it might be, permitted them to stand alone, to preserve their mental freedom without suffering it to degenerate into license.

Isolated from the reformed nations of which we have spoken, by natural position and political institutions, yet tracing their ancestry, in part at least, to the same source, speaking a kindred language, and stamped with many of the same characteristics, mental and physical, dwelt a people destined to exercise, through their arts and their arms, through the extent of their commerce and their colonies, an influence more potent than ever belonged to any other. Rome boasted that she gave laws to one world; England has planted the seed of her free institutions in two—seed which has sent its firm roots deep and wide into the heart of earth. And by what wonderful arrangements of an all-governing Power, was this people moulded for their work? With the brave old Briton, whose undisciplined valor left the Roman legions little to boast in their conquest, must unite the thoughtful spirit of the German, and to these must be added the fiery soul of the Norman, himself a compound of the rude, stern, all-subduing North, with the quick, gay, brilliant influences of sunny France, ere the metal shall be rightly tempered from which that mould is cast. The result has been a people whose deep thoughts are the parents of great actions; who, to the profound reasoning of the German, add the quick action of the Frenchman; who apply every idea to the purposes of practical life, and who therefore used the arms which had freed them from spiritual despotism, to win for themselves political liberty, denying the divine right of the king over their bodies and estates, as well as of the Pope over their souls.

From this nation proceeded the American people. We are the offspring, not of their immature youth, not of their feeble age, but of the strength of their manhood, when they had attained their fullest development, and when that development, untouched by one symptom of decay, still gave promise of immortality. The old Northman seemed to have roused himself from the slumber of ages, as our ancestors turned from the smiling shores of England to seek new homes in unknown lands across the sea. They came with loftier objects than Northman ever knew, and animated by holier hopes than ever beamed upon his spirit. Before we depict those objects, or refer to those hopes, let us recall the principles already asserted, and ask, whether the nation thus carefully prepared and providentially brought hither, had no peculiar work to do? Perhaps, from the circumstances attending their formation into a distinct people, and the peculiar forms thus impressed upon their social and political life, this work may be deduced. We will seek for it there; and we will endeavor, therefore, in the next chapter rapidly to sketch these circumstances and forms.

CHAPTER IV.

FEUDALISM AND ITS CONSEQUENCES.

In glancing rapidly over the governments of the old world, we find everywhere one principle appearing under forms variously modified by the characteristics of the people and the countries over which they have been established. This principle is feudalism, from which all these governments grew up. Trace them back to their earliest beginnings, and we arrive ever at some military chieftain, whose right was the product of his might, gathering about him his more peaceful or more feeble neighbors, and purchasing their fealty by his protection. The diffusion of Christianity and the establishment of law have, in many countries, broken down the original forms of feudalism and crippled its gigantic power, yet it still lives.

Fortified castles with portcullis and drawbridge, walls bristling with spears, and dungeons to which the light of day never enters, no longer frown defiance from every cliff, or look down with proud superiority on the humble hut of the artisan which has sought safety in its shadow, or the peaceful abode of the burgher, who must lay on its threshold a large portion of the wealth purchased by many toils as a peace-offering for the possession of the remainder. But the descendants of those who held those castles still claim the land that lay around them for many a mile, thus concentrating in the hands of a few the fair earth which God created for all; while on this far-extended surface hundreds, made of the same clay and deriving their life from the same divine source, labor unceasingly from dawn to dark to supply luxuries to the owner of the soil, and to themselves and their families the merest necessaries of an existence little elevated above that of the brute. Even in Christian England—England, which we honor for its noble institutions, and love as the land in which our fathers first drew breath, as the land which has given us laws and language, and from whose literature our spiritual life has been drawn—even in England this deadly Upas has diffused its baleful influence; feudalism is still the vital principle of many of her institutions, and reappears perpetually in her life, political and social. We see this with pain, and admit it with reluctance, for the spirit of feudalism is so opposed to the spirit of Christianity, that we cannot resist the conviction that as the latter triumphs, the former, and all to which it gives life, must be destroyed. Let us hope that in England this will be but as the wood and hay and stubble which may be burned, and leave the gold and silver and precious stones unharmed.

"No principle has long held influence over the popular mind which did not embody some truth," says a distinguished writer, and feudalism offers no exception to the rule. Honor to the brave hearts and the strong hands, which, "when there was no law were a law unto themselves," and won lands, and lordships, and fair renown, by aiding the weak, defending the innocent, and punishing the oppressor. There was truth in them, and well might the feeble seek to dwell within their shadow, and the industrious artizan and tradesman give something of their gains to those who, to secure to them the quiet possession of the remainder—

> "Slept with heads upon the sword
> Their fevered hands must grasp in waking."

But with the sovereignty of law this aspect of feudalism has passed away. The artisan and tradesman no longer need a defender—the law spreads her ægis over them, and secures to them the possession of their gains, —the produce of their toil. The same law, with impartial hand, protects the earl or duke in the lands and lordship which his father won. Well for this earl or duke it may be, that the price by which they were held,—the protection of the weak and the defence of the land in which he dwells,—are no longer claimed, for alas! strong hands and brave hearts are not always, like lands and lordships, transmissible by descent.

We would not be understood to assert that there are not those who use the power and property which they owe to the old feudalism for good—who obey the Christian law of benevolence, so far as they can without relinquishing the rights of their birth and station and thus breaking up the very foundations of the society in which they dwell, and whose peace and welfare they are bound to seek. Such, could this page meet their eye, would probably be the first to feel and to acknowledge with us, that feudalism and the wide and permanent distinctions in society which have grown out of it, are so far inconsistent with the spirit of that gospel which proclaims everywhere, "Love your neighbor as yourself"—"All ye are brethren"—that it renders obedience to its laws more difficult. Distinctions there will be indeed, while one has ten talents, another five, and another only one committed to him. While the laws established by God remain unchanged, the idle and dissolute father must leave his offspring to reap the bitter fruits of his acts in poverty and disgrace, and the industry, temperance, and integrity, of our progenitors, secure for us a vantage-ground in the race of life. But these distinctions are open to all—they stimulate therefore the efforts of all—they say not to any, "Stand aside, you may not enter here as a competitor." Widely differing from these are the distinctions which feudalism has bequeathed to every nation in which it has existed. There the distinctions are not of the various grades of talent, but of the common clay and the fine porcelain, the folly of the last being more excellent than the wisdom of the first. There we have classes privileged to live on the labor of others, to eat their bread in the sweat not of their own, but of their neighbors' brows,—escaping the sentence pronounced in Eden, by laying on their fellows their share of the burden which it was designed that all should bear. The hut there must be poorer that the palace may be richer. Again we say, that all this is diametrically opposed to the spirit of Christianity, which teaches the brotherhood of all men.

But while we thus see the wrongs which have become inextricably intertwined with all institutions based upon feudalism, let it not be thought that we are of those who could ruthlessly sweep those institutions from the earth. They are as structures venerable for age, and associated with all which we regard as most hallowed in the past. In these associations, and in their picturesque beauty, they possess a charm for the heart and the imagination which cannot be effaced by their utter unsuitableness to the present aspects of life. We shall mourn their downfall, come when it will. We cannot spare even one leaf of the ivy which is destroying while it decorates them. Yet "we rejoice with joy unspeakable" that the great Ruler of the earth has permitted other structures to be erected free from these dangerous decorations—other institutions to arise from which these wrongs have been excluded. Such we conceive to be the government of the United States of North America, whose earliest settlement was a protest against feudalism, with all its train of abuses in church and state. We are thus brought to the object of the present chapter, viz: a sketch of the circumstances under which these states were settled, and of the peculiar forms impressed on their goverment.

In saying that the earliest settlement in the United States was a protest against feudalism and its attendant abuses, we did not mean to deny that attempts had been made to settle here from other and less noble motives. The haughtiest and most despotic of the Tudors yet reigned over a submissive people, when the first unfortunate colony was planted on the Roanoke by the chivalrous Raleigh; and the absurdities and petty tyranny of the first and meanest of the Stuarts had not yet roused the English mind to resistance against hereditary power, when the little band into which the spirit of the adventurous Smith alone infused endurance, landed in Virginia, and marked their homage to their liege lord, by giving to the noble river up which they sailed, and to the town which they planted on its banks, the name of James. But the first of these colonies vanished from the earth, leaving no trace behind them, almost as soon as they were left by their commander, and the last lingered on in a state which daily threatened extinction, till the stern necessities of their position, and the ignorance and narrow policy of their patrons abroad, had forced them into a freer and more self-relying life. From mutual hardships and mutual aid sprang the spirit of true brotherhood and equality, and the government, throwing off its aristocratic and feudal forms, became free and popular, and in its freedom found strength,—then, and not till then, firmly rooting itself in the American soil. The next who sought our shores were the Puritans, who, driven by persecution from their homes in England, found a refuge first in Holland, and then on the bleak and rock-bound shores of New England. The despotic authority of the king or feudal lord, and of the bishop appointed by him, they denied in the very act of coming hither, and though they long continued to cling to England as their own and their fathers' home, it is impossible to read their simple narration of their voyage and their landing, of their early attempts at government, and the manner in which the various difficulties they encountered were met, without recognising in that small community the germ of the present republic of these United States. They then emphatically declared by their actions, what more than one hundred and fifty years after their descendants expressed in words:—"We are, and of right ought to be, free and independent." It is true they imperfectly understood the extent of those principles on which they acted, as they proved by not allowing to others the same freedom which they claimed for themselves. They were still but on the threshold of the temple of liberty which they were one day to enter, and the gates of which, having once entered, they would throw open to the world. From them went forth Roger Williams, the Baptist. The sect to which he belonged bears at this day the stigma of being the most narrow and bigotted among those who call themselves by the Christian name, yet they were in truth the first to set the world the example of perfect religious toleration. In the laws framed for that society which planted itself on Narraganset Bay, in what is now the little state of Rhode Island, Jew and Pagan, Mahomedan and Christian, might each worship the Universal Father in the mode dictated by his own conscience, while this mode did not interfere with the rights of others. The same large spirit of toleration appeared in the Roman Catholic Lord Baltimore, who, in the constitution prepared for the colonists of Maryland, placed worshippers of every Christian faith on perfect political equality. Pennsylvania and South Carolina were, like Massachusetts, settled, at least in part, by those who were seeking a refuge from religious and political oppression. Little attachment to the arbitrary institutions under whose sway they had suffered, could be supposed to live in the hearts of the

Quakers of England or the Huguenots of France. The first inhabitants of New York were Hollanders—a people more republican two hundred years ago, than now—and when it passed under the dominion of England, little change was made in its government. Georgia alone, of all the Atlantic states, was settled under the immediate auspices of royalty, and there, as in Virginia, it was not till the colony had ceased to look abroad for support, till it had become self-relying, and had so modified its original institutions as to give equal rights to all, that it began to prosper. Thus, by seemingly fortuitous circumstances, in which the devout mind recognises an overruling Providence, in some cases *without*, and, in some cases even *against* the design of the colonists themselves, the settlements made in that part of North America called the United States, were moulded into forms calculated to foster the spirit of equality, of brotherhood,—while each generation, as it passed, has done its part towards sweeping away the faint traces of the old feudalism which lingered amongst us. See here, then, the wide difference between our civilization and that of every other Christian nation—feudalism lying at the root of all their institutions, and intertwining itself with their very life.

We will not deny that we have lost some desirable things in our progress. Our life is not and cannot be so picturesque as that on which the old feudal times have impressed their imposing forms. No palaces, with their broad parks, their waving banners, and battlemented towers—no old cathedral, with its fretted roofs and "long-drawn aisles," the work of many generations, may rear their stately heads upon our hill sides, or in our flowery vales. No monarch, with diadem and sceptre—no nobles, with gorgeous robes, and all the glittering insignia of rank, dignify and adorn our social life—no prelate with flowing vestments, uniting in his person sanctions human and Divine—the power of the church and of the state—claims our homage. We have thus lost, with much that charms the eye, the highest visible representatives of earthly majesty and of spiritual supremacy. And in losing these, we incur the hazard of a much more serious loss. Some of the noblest properties of our nature have been exercised by the very inequalities we have condemned and discarded. Such are the loyalty which clings with unshaken determination to the object of its faith, amid disaster, and even in ruin—and the reverence which does homage to nobleness of spirit and purity of soul in their visible types. It is true that these qualities, in their highest development, demand no visible representative of the sublime ideals to which they attach themselves—that reverence bows with a purer and more self-abasing prostration before the majesty of virtue and the beauty of holiness, than before the mitred head and spotless lawn—and that loyalty is more intact when exercised in the defence of an unchanging principle, than of any human, and therefore fallible, embodiment of that principle. But it is also true, that, while the earthly, with its loud trumpet-calls and imposing shows, commands the attention of all, comparatively few are capable of that vigorous effort necessary to keep the mind awake to the claims of the unseen and spiritual, with its "still, small voice;" and thus the loyalty and the reverence yielded to nothing else, may become forgotten things.

Lest we should seem by these admissions to give too great a triumph to the opponents of our institutions, let us add, that if we have no splendid palaces, we have no huts green with damp and mouldering with decay; if we have no cathedrals which wake the world's wonder by their vastness and the elaborate style of their architecture, we have few, if any, villages in our land where at least one slender spire does not attract the eye and the thoughts Heavenward. Let it be understood also, that we do not admit a *necessity* for the sacrifice, under our equalizing institutions, of any quality essential to the perfection of our nature. There is danger, as we have said, of such sacrifices; but the danger may be averted—by what means we will endeavor to show hereafter.

CHAPTER V.

SOCIAL LIFE IN THE UNITED STATES.

FROM the forests of Germany, from the foaming seas of the North; through sunny France and England, noble England, our Fatherland, we have been led hither and have been built up into a nation; the first in the world's history which has been reared on ground unencumbered by old superstititions, and which has had for its corner-stone a perfect civil and religious liberty. Hither *have we been led,* and here have we *been* built up; for not by our own might or power, but by that of the living God was the work accomplished. Vain indeed would boasting be in us, for, like the Israelites of old, "we were led by a way we knew not of." It was under the influence of English life that our fathers grew into the stature of perfect men. They were Englishmen when refusing to submit their consciences to the dictation of any human power, they came here to establish as Americans that perfect liberty which as Englishmen they had conceived and loved, but which they knew it would be impossible to enjoy in a country into whose soil feudalism had struck its roots so deeply, that it must be the work of many years, perhaps of centuries, to extirpate them without danger to the noble edifices erected upon them. To us, their children, it belonged to complete what they had commenced, to fill up the fair outline which they had sketched, and to show the world the beauty of that Christian freedom with whose ideal they had become enamored, and in pursuit of which they had adventured and endured so much.

And how have we fulfilled this duty? In our political life, nobly. He who giveth wisdom hath made our counsellors wise; for our national acts have been, with few exceptions, marked by that sturdy common sense derived from our parent stock, and by that devotion to liberty to which we owe our existence as a distinct people.

But while such has been the aspect of our political life, far different has been that of our social life. As a nation independent, self-relying, and moving onward with a calmness marking just confidence in our powers, and a hearty conviction of the truth of our principles; in social life we have been servile imitators, the apes of every folly, and apologists of every vice to which European custom has given a sanction.

And whence springs this great difference? Is it not that—while American statesmen, those who preside over our national acts, have understood their position, and, having a definite aim, have advanced to its accomplishment with assured steps—American women, those who preside over social life, have understood neither their present position nor the future to which they are tending, and therefore have moved on without any definite aim, "wandering clouds, carried hither and thither by every wind" of fashion?

And must it be thus? Is there not for us too a work to do, a destiny to accomplish? May not we, the women of America, mould our social life by our intelligent convictions into a form which shall make it the fit handmaid of our political life in its grand simplicity and lofty aims? If we would accomplish this, one thing is evident—so evident that it can scarcely require either argument or persuasion to commend it to the acceptance of every intelligent mind—it is, that we are to look elsewhere than to Europe for the model after which we are to work. The social life we find there may be imposing in its grandeur, beautiful in its refinements, and gorgeous in its adornments to the eye of him who looks only on its surface, but it cannot be made to harmonize with the principles on which our political life, our very existence as an independent nation, is founded.

This is, we repeat, a fact so obvious, that it cannot fail to be accepted as truth by every intelligent mind. But something more than the mind's acceptance is necessary to give to any truth that living power which makes it grow and bring forth fruit; it must be received into the heart, and against this truth, we fear, our hearts are still closed. We are endeavoring to reconcile the irreconcilable; and offer to the world, at present, the appearance of architects who, having commenced a grand and noble edifice in the simple Doric style, are striving to ingraft upon their original plan the graceful decorations of the Corinthian. Each style has a beauty of its own, but the two united would produce only a grotesque absurdity. Yet more striking would the absurdity be, if, as in our own case, the resources of the architects were too restricted to permit them to give the decorations at which they aimed in all their richness and elegance, obliging them to content themselves with such a poor seeming as could satisfy only the most superficial and most inartistic observer. Such must be our imitation of the social life of those countries in which the whole landed property was originally distributed amongst a few leaders, and where the law of entail has confined the succession to this property, with almost all the wealth accumulated from it by centuries of careful cultivation, to nearly the original number.

What is it amongst us which excites that ridicule from foreigners, under which we have so often winced? Is it the simplicity of our political organization, the plainness of our citizen-president, the unostentatious home provided for his abode, and the unceremonious reception which, as the representative of a republican people, he gives to the representatives of other lands? Is it the academies and colleges, so much less liberally endowed than their own, and wanting all that prestige, the richest legacy of the past, with which time has hallowed the halls of Oxford and of Cambridge? Is it the comparatively small extent of our cities, or their want of splendid architectural adornments? No, in some of these things, if indeed they are persons possessing the faculty of vision, they see that beautiful consistency of practice and principle which all men honor; and in others they are ready to acknowledge that the wonder is not that so little, but that so much has been done; not that the result of two hundred years' labor here has not equalled that of two thousand years abroad, but that it has made so near an approximation to it. But when they turn to our social life, to its feverish ambition, its mean jealousies, its ostentatious displays, its fretful sensitiveness, its strange contrasts, its want of all harmony and beauty, of all repose and dignity, their respect for us vanishes, and the kindliest feeling which can succeed, is compassion for our vain struggles after the unattainable.

Let it not be thought that we would so belie our country as to insinuate that this is *all* which our social life presents; but this is what lies on the surface, this, ever eager for exhibition, starts forward and is first seen by foreigners—*first* and often *only* seen. Often this class presents all of society into which foreigners enter; and this, with uneducated laborers and the heterogeneous mixture of enterprising industry and despairing indolence, of vice and misery, yearly received from Europe, makes up the sum of what they denominate American society. Into the true American life, the life in which labor and refinement walk hand in hand, in which, with a thorough understanding of themselves and their position, a class, intelligent, educated, and often even highly accomplished, having set before them an ideal nobler than any yet attained on earth, are working out that ideal in the quietness of spirits dwelling in too high a region to be disturbed by the capricious winds and currents of fashion; into this life they have never entered, they know nothing of its existence, and if some one from it crosses their path, he is but an individual, an exception to general rules, his excellencies belong to him as man—the shades, by which in the best those excellencies will be darkened, are American.

Let us not complain of this as unjust. These "second Daniels" are but men, and judge, as we would do, by what they see and hear, forgetting that not in the thunder and the tempest, but in the still, small voice, dwells the spirit and the power. For them and for the world, at least the world among ourselves, to whom it is of most importance, let us endeavor to lift the veil from this true American life. Happy shall we be if we can so reveal its beauty that those who look shall love and strive to make it theirs.

CHAPTER VI.

SOCIAL EVILS—WOMAN THEIR REFORMER.

It has been often repeated, so often that many have grown weary of the repetition, that one of the first principles of our government is equality; and yet it may be doubted whether some among us would not find it difficult to define what this equality means, or in what it consists. Not, surely, in personal qualities; for none can be so besotted as to imagine, that by simply being Americans, they may claim equality with all of the same nation in the dignities conferred by high moral or intellectual power. Nor does it consist in an equal participation in all the advantages which wealth and social position confer; for should any one claim this and attempt to enforce his claim, the bolts of a prison or a madhouse would soon teach him that the opinion of the world was adverse to his own.

And yet it is not a vain boast, that we did first, as a people, assert, and have striven to maintain, that all men were born free and equal,—with equal right to enjoy and to improve to the utmost, that heritage derived, under Providence, from their progenitors.

Was thy father a builder of other men's houses—a shoemaker, working at his last—or a blacksmith, wielding the hammer with sturdy arm—and did he, by his honest industry, win for thee, his loved one, a higher, and in the world's judgment, a better fortune? Let him smile as he looks at thy boyish sports, and say to himself—"Thy life shall be of a nobler sort than mine." It shall be thine own fault if this saying prove not prophetic. There is no seminary of learning in the land into which his gold may not buy thee admittance, and there thou shalt stand on such eminence as thy merits shall command. From such seminary thou mayst pass into the profession that best pleases thee; all are open to thee, and that prophetic father may live to see thee a judge on the bench of the Supreme Court, a senator in the halls of Congress, or a President of the United States. No privileged class shall say to thee—"Touch not that honor—set not thy foot upon that eminence; it belongs to us." Thou art free; free to develop thyself as thy will shall prompt, and thy powers permit. This world is God's world, and He hath given thee so much of it as thou, with thy best faculties, canst conquer. Such is the language of our Constitution, to which nothing in our political life gives denial. There the cloth of frieze stands unrepulsed beside the cloth of gold, and may even attain to a higher position; but not thus is it with our social life. There, the intellect may glow with man's noblest powers, the heart throb with his highest aspirations, and the manners may reflect, in their gentleness and refinement, the glory of such powers and such aspirations; yet, if all this be covered by the cloth of frieze, away with it—it may not enter the charmed circle of "*good society,*" or enter only after its own degradation, as Samson, shorn of his locks, was brought before the lords of the Philistines to make sport for them.

And what constitutes this *soi disant* good society? Wealth, and the senseless fripperies which wealth may purchase. Oh! give us back the old reverence for a noble name. If we must have a privileged class—if we must bear "the contumely which patient merit of the unworthy takes," restore to us the illusion by which we might fancy ourselves doing homage to the kingly spirits of earth in the persons of their degenerate descendants. In such homage there may be something ennobling; but in this worship of Mammon, this bending the spirit to vulgarity and frivolity, because decorated with jewels and brocade, there is every thing debasing. And to what do we owe the strength of this sentiment of veneration for wealth amongst us? Is it not to our having placed before us the social life of Europe as our model? We cannot command domains associated with ancestral names whose very sound is a spell, stirring the heart like a trumpet-tone, and evoking images of past splendor which throw a halo over ruin and decay; but wealth will enable us to build houses almost as large as those to which these domains are attached, and a great deal finer. Base and shaft to our Corinthian column may be wanting; but we will place the rich capital upon our Doric base, and by covering its decorations with gold-leaf, make it much more showy.

If we would cease to be the world's derision—if we would take the position which God designed us to take among the nations of the earth, we must put from us this low ambition, we must understand our noble work, and elevate our aims to its accomplishment.

Feudalism had its mission—a mission to educate men into reverence and obedience. The rude, semi-barbarous nations of Europe in the middle ages could not have appreciated the majesty of law, and would neither have reverenced nor obeyed a power so spiritual. These emotions, then, must be excited in their minds by that physical force, and those outward demonstrations of superiority, which strike the senses. The diadem, sparkling with gems, the purple robe, the golden sceptre, all the insignia of royal or of noble rank, all the rigid etiquette which marked the gradations of society, and kept each class hedged in as by an insuperable barrier, which was soon made to appear a divine and indefeasible right—these were all but means towards the accomplishment of this end. That they were wisely-appointed and successful means, we may learn by a glance at the history of the civilized world. Let us take England, the most advanced in Christian civilization of all those nations whose barbarous or semi-barbarous origin required these educational processes. While at every advancing step she has made, some form has been discarded, or has, at least, ceased to awaken the public reverence, has not the inner spirit which that form had represented, the law, been more clearly revealed—winning, in its majestic simplicity, a truer and more enduring homage than had been yielded to its imposing representative? There was a period in her history—the memorable period of the Stuart dynasty—when the forms and the spirit, royalty and the law whose power it had been created to represent and to enforce, were arrayed against each other, and the result proved that forms were fast becoming useless to a nation which had learned well its lesson of reverence to the spirit of law.

Yet, though their work was well nigh done, their use had well nigh passed away, these forms must be reconciled to the spirit of law, not discarded, for they were but branches of that feudalism from which the whole social structure had grown up. They must not be torn away, lest that structure should be shaken to the base; they must be left to the action of time. Slowly, but surely, they will decay and fall away of themselves.

And may it not be that in the neglect of the principles which have thus guided the English people, has arisen the ill-success which has hitherto marked all other European revolutions. The first French revolution, and those lately occurring in some other European nations, released from all the checks and restraints of outward forms those who had been so held down by sheer, physical force, that their dwarfed minds and palsied hearts had room for no emotions but those of selfish terror or mad revenge. No reverence for God or man stayed their fierce hands as, seizing on these feelings, the demagogue of the hour swayed them hither or thither at his will. Their gross senses could not appreciate the force of the subtle spirit of law, their obedience could be obtained only by the exhibition of material power, and thus the institutions, on which their whole social life rested, were torn away root and branch at one time, only to be built up on the same basis in succeeding years. But the English revolution, if the name of revolution may indeed be given to that contest which ended with a change of dynasty in England, was begun, continued, and ended in a spirit of reverence for the law; and this reverence made the victorious party wisely careful not to touch one institution which had become associated with the law. "As our revolution was a vindication of ancient rights, so it was conducted with strict attention to ancient formalities," says Macaulay, in that masterly work which has left us little to learn in relation to this period of English history.

And why was it that not till our ancestors had entered on this great contest, did one of the many attempts made to plant English colonies on these shores prove successful? Was it that they had now reached the culminating point of their education in the love of liberty and reverence for law; that beyond this their advance was stayed by the very arrangements which had been necessary to their safe development so far; that to attain to a more perfect external development of their own noble principles, they must be transplanted to a new soil, and begin afresh the race of life, free from those impediments whose demolition, where they have once existed, must ever be attended with danger of anarchy and misrule? Was it that here, on the basis of Christian institutions and equal rights, we might find it easier to construct that fair temple which has for its foundation and its corner-stone, "Love God supremely, and your neighbor, whether he be king or beggar, as yourself?" We believe it was, and we would ask, why have we made so little advance towards this highest attainment in human association? The answer to this question must be found, we think, in the fact already noted, that the principles which we have politically asserted, we have socially denied; striving to establish socially the inequalities against which we have politically rebelled, only substituting for the distinctions of birth those created by wealth.

In the rapid glance which we have taken of the various influences that have combined to form the English character, we have seen a nation happily "compounded of every nation's best," trained to reverence of law and love of liberty. In America we have seen this same people taking a position in which that reverence for law remained the only restraint upon their actions; in which, therefore, they were free in the best sense of the word, free even as God made man, free from all restraint but that which, at the command of an enlightened conscience, he imposes on himself. To those who have followed us in this sketch, and who, assenting to the proposition, that each creature in the Providence of God finds itself in that condition for which it is peculiarly fitted, and may thus discover in its offices the exact correlatives of its powers,—these powers being the sum of its natural capabilities, and of the circumstances under which these capabilities have been exercised and developed,—also think, with us, that while man has been endowed with qualities which render him the proper controller of the outward machinery of government, the thews and sinews of society, woman is by nature equally fitted to preside over its inner spirit, over the homes from which the social as distinguished from the political life must be derived; the conclusion must, it seems to us, be irresistible, that to American women we must look to rectify the errors of American society, and that from them we may hope to derive a life freer from factitious distinctions, controlled more by enlightened convictions and less by conventional forms, a life nobler, more spiritual, more in conformity with Christian principles than any the world has yet seen. To such a work are we now endeavoring to awaken the attention of our countrywomen. It is a noble work: a work which, we think, they must themselves acknowledge to be worthy the exercise of all their powers.

Permit us, in illustration of our subject, to place before you a sketch of an American woman of fashion as she is and as she might be—as she *must* be to accomplish the task we would appoint her. Examine with a careful eye "the counterfeit presentment" of these two widely differing characters, and choose the model on which you will form yourselves. And first, by a few strokes of this magic wand—the pen—we will conjure within the charmed circle of your vision, the woman of fashion as she is.

Flirtilla,—for so noted a character must not want a name,—may well be pronounced a favorite of nature and of fortune. To the first she owed a pleasing person and a mind which offered no unapt soil for cultivation; by favor of the last, she was born the heiress to wealth and to those advantages which wealth unquestionably confers. Her childhood was carefully sequestered from all *vulgar* influences, and she was early taught, that to be a *little lady* was her highest possible attainment. At six years old she astonished the *élite* assembled in her father's halls, and even dazzled the larger assemblages of Saratoga by her grace in dancing and by the ease with which she conversed in French, which, as it was the language of her nursery attendants, had been a second mother-tongue to her. At the fashionable boarding-school, at which her education was, in common parlance, *completed,* she distanced all competitors for the prizes in modern languages, dancing, and music; and acquired so much acquaintance with geography and history as would secure her from mistaking Prussia for Persia, or imagining that Lord Wellington had conquered Julius Cæsar—in other words, so much knowledge of them as would guard her from betraying her ignorance. To these acquirements she added a slight smattering of various natural sciences. All these accomplishments had nearly been lost to the world, by her forming an attachment for one of fine qualities, personal and mental, who was entirely destitute of fortune. From the fatal mistake of yielding to such an attachment she was preserved by a judicious mother, who placed before her in vivid contrast the commanding position in which she would be placed as the wife of Mr. A—, with his houses and lands, his bank stock and magnificent equipage; and the *médiocre* station she would occupy as Mrs. B—, a station to which one of her aspiring mind could not readily succumb, even though she found herself there in company with one of the most interesting and agreeable of men. Relinquishing with a sigh the gratification of the last sentiment that bound her to nature and to rational life, she magnanimously sacrificed her inclinations to her sense of duty, and became Mrs. A—. From this time her course has been undisturbed by one faltering feeling, one wavering thought. She has visited London and Paris, only that she might assure herself that her house possessed all which was considered essential to a *genteel* establishment in the first, and that her toilette was the most *recherché* that could be obtained in the last. She laughs at the very idea of wearing any thing made in America, and is exceedingly merry over the portraitures of Yankee character and Yankee life occasionally to be met in the pages of foreign tourists, or to be seen personated in foreign theatres. She complains much of the promiscuous character of American society, dances in no set but her own, and, in order to secure her exclusiveness from contact with the common herd, moves about from one point of fashionable life to another, attended by the same satellites, to whom she is the great centre of attraction. Her manners, like her dresses, are imported from Paris. She talks and laughs very loudly at all public places, lectures, concerts, and the like ; and has sometimes, even in the house of God, expressed audibly her assent with or dissent from the preacher, that she may prove herself entirely free from that shockingly American *mauvaise honte,* which she supposes to be all that keeps other women silent. Any gentleman desiring admission to her circle must produce authentic credentials that he has been abroad, must wear his mustaches after the latest Parisian cut, must interlard his bad English with worse French, and must be familiar with the names and histories of the latest ballet-dancers and opera-singers who have created a fever of excitement abroad. To foreigners she is particularly gracious, and nothing throws her into such a fervor of activity as the arrival in the country of an English Lord, a German Baron, or a French or Italian Count. To draw such a character within her circle she thinks no effort too great, no sacrifice of feeling too humiliating.

It may be objected that all our descriptions of the fashionable woman as she is, relates to externals; that of the essential character, the inner life, we have, in truth, said nothing. But what can we do? So far as we have yet been able to discover, this class is destitute of any inner life. Those who compose it live for the world and in the world. Home is with them only the place in which they receive visits. We acknowledge that few in our country have yet attained to so perfect a development of fashionable character as we have here described; but to some it is already an attainment; to many—we fear to *most*, young women of what are called the higher classes in our large cities—it is an aim. Nobler spirits there are, indeed, among us, of every age and every class, and from these we must choose our example of a woman of fashion as she should be. On her, too, we will bestow a name—a name associated with all gentle and benignant influences—the name of her who in her shaded retreats received of old the ruler of earth's proudest empire, that she might "breathe off with the holy air" of her pure affection, "that dust o' the heart" caught from contact with coarser spirits. So have we dreamed of Egeria, and Egeria shall be the name of our heroine. Heroine indeed, for heroic must be her life. With eyes uplifted to a protecting Heaven, she must walk the narrow path of right, —a precipice on either hand,—never submitting in her lowliness of soul, to the encroachments of the selfish, and eager, and clamorous crowd,—never bowing her own native nobility to the dictation of those whom the world styles great. "Resisting the proud, but giving grace unto the humble," if we may without irreverence appropriate to a mortal, words descriptive of Him whose unapproachable and glorious holiness we are exhorted to imitate.

In society, Egeria is more desirous to please than to shine. Her associates are selected mainly for their personal qualities, and if she is peculiarly attentive and deferential to any class, it is to those unfortunates whom poverty, the accidents of birth, or the false arrangements of society, have divorced from a sphere for which their refinement of taste and manner and their intellectual cultivation had fitted them. Admission to her society is sought as a distinction, because it is known that it must be purchased by something more than a graceful address, a well-curled mustache, or the reputation of a travelled man. At her entertainments, you will often meet some whom you will meet nowhere else; some promising young artist, yet unknown to fame,—some who, once standing in the sunshine of fortune, were well known to many whose vision is too imperfect for the recognition of features over which adversity has thrown its shadow. The influence of Egeria is felt through the whole circle of her acquaintance;—she encourages the young to high aims and persevering efforts,—she brightens the fading light of the aged, but above all is she a blessing and a glory within her own home. Her husband cannot look on her—to borrow Longfellow's beautiful thought—without "reading in the serene expression of her face, the Divine beatitude, 'Blessed are the pure in heart.'" Her children revere her as the earthly type of perfect love. They learn even more from her example than her precept, that they are to live not to themselves, but to their fellow-creatures, and to God in them. She has so cultivated their taste for all which is beautiful and noble, that they cannot but desire to conform themselves to such models. She has taught them to love their country and devote themselves to its advancement—not because it excels all others, but because it is that to which God in his providence united them, and whose advancement and true interest they are bound to seek by all just and Christian methods. In a word, she has never forgotten that they were immortal and responsible beings, and this thought has reappeared in every impression she has stamped upon their minds.

But it is her conduct towards those in a social position inferior to her own, which individualizes most strongly the character of Egeria. Remembering that there are none who may not, under our free institutions, attain to positions of influence and responsibility, she endeavors, in all her intercourse with them, to awaken their self-respect and desire for improvement, and she is ever ready to aid them in the attainment of that desire, and thus to fit them for the performance of those duties that may devolve on them.

"Are you not afraid that Bridget will leave you, if, by your lessons, you fit her for some higher position?" asked a lady, on finding her teaching embroidery to a servant who had shown much aptitude for it.

"If Bridget can advance her interest by leaving me, she shall have my cheerful consent to go. God forbid that I should stand in the way of good to any fellow-creature—above all, to one whom, by placing her under my temporary protection, he has made it especially my duty to serve," was her reply.

In the general ignorance and vice of the population

daily pouring into our country from foreign lands, Egeria finds new reason for activity, in the moral and intellectual advancement of all who are brought within her sphere of influence.

Egeria has been accused of being ambitious for her children. "I am ambitious for them," she replies; "ambitious that they should occupy stations that may be as a vantage-ground from which to act for the public good."

Notwithstanding this ambition, she has, to the astonishment of many in her own circle, consented that one of her sons should devote himself to mechanics. She was at first pitied for this, as a mortification to which she must certainly have been compelled, by her husband's singular notions, to submit.

"You mistake," said Egeria, to one who delicately expressed this pity to her; "my son's choice of a trade had my hearty concurrence. I was prepared for it by the whole bias of his mind from childhood. He will excel in the career he has chosen, I have no doubt; for he has abilities equal to either of his brothers, and he loves the object to which he has devoted them. As a lawyer or physician he would, probably, have but added one to the number of *médiocre* practitioners who lounge through life with no higher aim than their own maintenance."

"But then," it was objected, "he would not have sacrificed his position in society."

Egeria is human, and the sudden flush of indignation must have crimsoned the mother's brow at this; and somewhat of scorn, we doubt not, was in the smile that curled her lip as she replied, "My son can afford to lose the acquaintance of those who cannot appreciate the true nobility and independence of spirit which have made him choose a position offering, as he believes, the highest means of development for his own peculiar powers, and the greatest probability, therefore, of his becoming useful to others."

Our sketches are finished—imperfect sketches we acknowledge them. It would have been a labor of love to have rendered the last complete—to have followed the steps of Egeria—the Christian gentlewoman—through at least one day of her life; to have shown her embellishing her social circle by her graces of manner and charms of conversation, and to have accompanied her from the saloons which she thus adorned, to more humble abodes. In these abodes she was ever a welcome as well as an honored guest, for she bore thither a respectful consideration for their inmates, which is a rarer and more coveted gift to the poor than any wealth can purchase. Having done this, we would have liked to glance at her in the tranquil evening of a life well spent, and to contrast her then with Flirtilla, old beyond the power of rouge, false teeth, and false hair, to disguise—still running through a round of pleasures that have ceased to charm, regretting the past, dissatisfied with the present, and dreading the future, alternately courting and abusing the world, which has grown weary of her. But to stray into these flowery paths of imagination, would lead us too far away from a graver purpose, to which we return.

CHAPTER VII.

CHRISTIAN CIVILIZATION.

As we have advanced in our argument, we have become more and more convinced, that the difference between the civilization we are endeavoring to portray, and that which has hitherto been the aim of nations the most advanced in intellectual and even in religious culture, is, that the former is a Christian civilization—a civilization which moulds the spirit into shapes of grace and beauty, and on these lays all external decorations, as a suitable drapery;—while the latter considers all spiritual education as a thing apart from itself, and is satisfied to conceal by a beautiful exterior the deformities which lie deep within. Let us not be accused of saying, that all nations before us have neglected spiritual education. From the low roofs beneath which peasant mothers lull their babes to sleep with Christian hymns, and from gorgeous cathedrals, whose vaulted roofs reverberate each day anthems of praise to the Most High,—from the "ragged schools" in which outcast children have been gathered by the most self-sacrificing philanthropists the world ever saw, and from those spacious colleges which have been for ages a nation's boast—would come voices of denial to a dogma so absurd, illiberal, and untrue. It is not of the lack of spiritual education in older lands that we complain, but that it has been a thing apart from their civilization, which might have been grafted as easily upon a Pagan as a Christian faith—nay, more easily, for where their religion and their civilization have met, they have met, not as friends, but as antagonists. Who in London or Paris would be thought to have attained to the highest degree of social refinement—she who, respecting the sanctity of those hours which God had marked as His own, and desiring to be "in the spirit on the Lord's day," should refuse to spend the evening of Saturday in amusements calculated to dissipate all serious thought, should make a point of conscience of a regular attendance on the services of the sanctuary, and of an earnest regard to those services—or she who thinks of Saturday only as the best night for the opera, and of Sunday as a day of *ennui* scarcely to be borne, were it not for the fashionable drive, more thronged on that than on other days, and for the succession of visiters whom she is too much engaged to receive during the week?

That to which we would exhort our countrywomen, is, to make the tree good that its fruit may be good, and its flowers and foliage enduring in their beauty, because sustained by an inner life. We would spare no true refinement, no external grace, from our plan of education. The nicely modulated voice, whose subtle melody steals sometimes to the heart wrapped in a thousand folds of selfishness—the gentle grace that wins regard—the modest dignity which commands respect from insolence itself—we would have them all; not as a dress to be worn on state occasions, but as an inseparable part of the person—the spontaneous developments of a living spirit. We may be told, with a smile, that we are revealing no new discovery in education, in thus marking the desirableness of a harmonious cultivation of all the powers—the spiritual as well as the physical—those of thought and feeling as well as of expression. To such a suggestion we would most respectfully reply, that the education of which we speak, is not that of the school or the pulpit, but that of society. And to produce such results, our social life must be something more than a wonderfully correct imitation, considering our small means, of the imposing life of other lands—it must be a true life, a *being,* not a *seeming.* Better the plainest and lowliest being, whose unattractive form shrouds a living spirit—who thinks, and speaks, and acts, from a self-directing impulse—than the loveliest statue ever modelled by the hand of man, though the skill of the artificer may have added to its beauty the powers of the automaton, in speech and action.

We have already endeavored to show what, even at the risk of wearying our readers, we must repeat, that the social arrangements we are imitating can only have life in the soil over which feudalism once spread its gigantic branches. They must be grafted on that stock to flourish. There they still have life and meaning. In countries whose population has increased beyond their resources, or whose resources are so apportioned, that, while the few live in a luxury we would vainly covet, the many must toil from light to dark, for food and raiment and shelter, there is meaning in those outward shows, which mark more emphatically than any law could do, to the brutish minds of the crowd, the majesty of their rulers. Where there are various orders in a state, on whose preservation the safety of that state depends, there is meaning and life even in the refinements and courtesies of polite society, apart from the spirit of him who practises them. These refinements and courtesies say to the brutish herd: "You are not of us; toil on through your wearisome day, and when night comes, sleep the unbroken sleep which comes only to the worker —rarely indeed to the thinker. We to whom knowledge has given power, we who bear about us, as you see, impressed on our brows, speaking through our lips, and manifesting itself in our every movement, the visible signs of that power—we will think for you, fight for you, and guard you from that anarchy, that universal warfare, into which, if deserted by us, in your ignorance and your wretchedness, you must fall, and which is worse than the worst despotism." And the more imposing the forms under which the life of the upper classes presents itself, the more impressive is the utterance of these dicta. But where there is freedom, where the people are their own rulers, society should assume a simpler aspect; for from the spirit of the people must it receive its character, so far as it is any thing more than a system of dead forms, a mere automaton.

And now, are we, the women of America, prepared

to say: "It shall be thus with us; our social life shall reflect the free, independent spirit of our people. The old American life, noble in its simplicity, shall not be stifled beneath a mass of foreign fripperies, meaningless to us at least. Understanding our mission, we will, with God's help, perform it. Sacrificing no refinement, relinquishing no grace, cherishing all the gentle courtesies of life as expressions of its cordial sympathies, we will not be tempted from the beautiful simplicity of our mothers, by the follies of a little circle of successful speculators—millionaires with heavy purses and light heads, who having found even their wealth insufficient to maintain the expenses of fashionable life in Europe, would establish a second-rate imitation of it here. Wealth, and its gifts of dress and equipage, shall not win us to countenance vice or to flatter folly. The simplest garb and most retired home shall not veil from our earnest search, or withdraw from our friendly circle, those whose virtue, intelligence, and refinement, make them worthy of our regard, and capable of sympathizing with our own high objects. While we look coldly upon those who would establish themselves in that circle, upon no better claim than that of wealth, too new to have won for its possessor even the superficial gloss which sometimes veils innate vulgarity; we will delight to hold out a helping hand to the poor scholar, who, with a mind rich in God's best gifts, is compelled to plod his weary way along thoroughfares thronged with the ignorant and the coarse, thirsting and thirsting in vain for companionship with the refined and cultivated. We will call to our side the gentle girl, who, even in the uncongenial atmosphere to which poverty has condemned her, cherishes her sympathies with all the refinements that embellish our lives; and, that these may stand beside us unshamed, we will keep those lives within the limits of an elegant simplicity. Denying ourselves nothing that will serve as means of culture, we will sacrifice, if need be, to such treasures, the vulgar love for personal decoration, or the mad search for gayeties, which would ill assort with the untroubled serenity of minds dwelling in a region elevated above the sensual. The generous hospitalities which were wont to characterize our homes, shall not be lessened, that we may appear in laces that a queen might wear, or jewels that would become a birth-night ball. A suit of diamonds shall have no charm for us, in comparison with a picture or a statue bearing the undying impress of the immortal mind from which it sprang. We will tread on carpets less soft than those woven by Persian looms, we will want the gilded cornice and the fretted roof, we will consent to relinquish the indisputable elegance of rose-wood and or-molu, if, by yielding these, we may secure that best room of all in a house, a spacious library, in which we may command at will the noblest powers of the noblest men of every age and every land—in which magic spells are stored, powerful to conjure before our dazzled vision scenes of such splendor as would make the realities of many a royal palace dim. Nor shall this be a selfish enjoyment. If, by this disposal of our wealth, we have denied ourselves the poor, mean triumph of outshining our neighbors in some butterfly ball, or of assembling our dear five hundred friends to gaze with envious hearts upon our tinsel splendor, we will invite all of them who have minds to prize our nobler treasures to enjoy them with us—especially will we bid to this 'feast of reason' those to whom a less favoring destiny has denied the power of gratifying such tastes. Thus, in our measure, will we work to cultivate and refine all around us, and to produce that only true equality, an equality of mind, without some approach to which a republic is a dream, and will pass like a dream away."

Equality of mind! Shall the workers of a nation—

the hard-handed men of toil become likewise men of thought? Here only of all the world—here, where labor is so well rewarded, where the necessaries of life are so easily obtained, and the diffusion of intelligence is so general—may these characters be united and man stand complete in every faculty. Every thing here tends to this desired consummation. Elihu Burritt has already taught us what one laboring man can do; while from our factories have gone forth contributions to our literature, conned amid the unceasing whirl of looms and spindles, not less valuable, to say the least, than many of the same class penned in the repose of the tasteful boudoir. The labor which accomplishes its ends without becoming so extreme as to exhaust the vital powers, stimulates our mental faculties, and brings them into fuller and healthier play. We shall have probably few learned pundits in our land, few men who live a life dissevered from that of the rest of the world—who would think more of the discovery of a long missing Greek folio than of a new continent—who would exult more at detecting in the language of some modern nation an undoubted relationship to that spoken ages ago in the forests of Germany, on the shores of the Black Sea, or amid the sands of the desert, than in catching the first notes of that hymn of universal freedom, which is one day to sound from shore to shore, and by the thrill it wakes in every human heart, to prove the brotherhood of all. *Our* learned men must still be living men. No princely patrons or rich endowments will enable them to live apart from their fellows. They, too, must work and grow weary, and refresh themselves at the fountain of all bright and pure thoughts—home—the home of mother, sister, wife. They, too, must learn through trial—through success painfully bought and suffering patiently endured—to sympathize with the common heart. Shall we mourn this? Shall we say, that with us, as there is no chief in the political world, so there will be none in letters—that in our land there will be no mountain peak from whose glow the nations shall first hail the coming dawn? To this we have but one answer—it was precisely in such a life of toil and suffering that Shakspeare and Milton were formed.

It is only, as we believe, in such an amalgamation of two classes hitherto held distinct—in such a fusing together, as it were, of labor with thought and refinement—that we shall attain to the perfect type of man. Even sinless man, over whose frame disease had no power, was not left wholly idle. He had

> "A pleasant labor, to reform
> The flowery arbors and the alleys green"

of Eden. To sinful man the first award of Infinite Wisdom and Love was, "By the sweat of thy brow shalt thou win thy bread;" and who that has looked with an observant eye and a reflecting mind on the face of the earth, has not felt that it was Love which dictated this award? "There is," says Carlyle, "a perennial nobleness and even sacredness in work." Heaven, we believe, is no place for the indulgence of sloth. Happy spirits, we doubt not, work, though their work, like that of the God-Man, is noble, and spiritual, and free, springing spontaneously from an impulse within, not constrained by external circumstances. To this we shall probably never attain on earth; but as we become elevated by intelligence and refinement, and, above all, by that love to God and love to man, which is the culminating point of all intelligence and all refinement, our work will doubtless make some approximation to the freedom, and the joyousness, and the nobility of angels' work. Already intelligence has done much to lessen the drudgery, the brutalizing influence of excessive labor; but the mechanical arts through which this has been accomplished, have been hitherto applied only to individual emolument;—

they have yet to receive a new and mightier impulse from Christian benevolence—from the desire to elevate to a nobler life, the whole human race.

We are not so Quixotic as to believe, that words of ours may prevail on the idle children of luxury to take their fair share of the world's labor, that their brothers may not sink beneath the burden forced on them. Still less can we hope to persuade them, that they would find the law of labor, within certain limits, a beneficent law in its action upon themselves. They would perhaps ask us, Shall we reject the services of those who depend on our payment of those services for bread, that we may have work for ourselves? We answer, Far from it; we would have you exact less for the payment you give, and make up the lack of service by your own exertion. Thus would you gain, perchance, health of mind and body, and your brother man some of that time which would be to him an invaluable boon, and which is to you often an intolerable burden.

As we have said, however, we have no hope of producing such an influence on the luxurious idler, and we would not waste our energies on a hopeless task. But there is another class, on the yet unhardened moulds of whose characters and destinies we would fain flatter ourselves that even our feeble words may fall with some good effect. Few familiar with our social life, can have failed to remark the number of young men among us seeking work and finding none, because, while their powers have never been trained to application in a defined line, they are unwilling to apply them in the only way in which undisciplined power may be used successfully—in real, manual labor. These young men are generally the sons of fathers possessing just wealth enough to maintain what is called, under the false social system we are combating, a *genteel* establishment. They have been born in luxurious homes, which the death of the father, and the consequent division of property, have dismantled. They are now left with no means of securing the expensive training necessary to the practice of either of the learned professions, and with ideas of life which forbid them to use their strength in the only way in which they could make it available for their support. Thus the best years of their lives—the very spring-tide of their powers—is wasted in hopeless inaction, and all manliness and independence of character is lost, while they sue and cringe to this patron and to that for aid to support their fading gentility, till, wearied by their importunities and disgusted with their servility, the very circle for which they have sacrificed all that was truly valuable in themselves, contemn and disown them.

To reform this great evil and to rectify those false views from which it springs—woman—woman, especially in that class which gives the tone to manners, may greatly if not chiefly contribute. Let her show that, in her opinion, labor imprints no brand upon the brow—that there shall be, with her consent, no social ban upon it—let her make her social life so simple that the laborer may partake it, if he have acquired the refinement necessary to place him in sympathy with it, and he will set this before him as a new and most influential motive for the exertion of every faculty. Still more, in that household which is her own peculiar realm, let her endeavor to awaken the dormant faculties of all around her. Let her never deny to the workers there some leisure for the cultivation of the spiritual part of their nature. Say not, were this generally done, we should soon have no servants. You will always have helpers in every department of labor,—for the poor we are assured we shall have always with us—and the more intelligent and refined these helpers, the better for us and for our children. Perchance you smile at the idea of refinement as connected with some acts of household necessity. Look abroad, scorner, over the length and breadth of the land, and see in what has art of late so manifested its power as in lessening the drudgery of the house-worker, and in taking from her office all that was offensive to good taste or incompatible with true refinement. We have adverted to these mechanical improvements in all labor, as promises of "a good time coming." It will surely come. Let us, women of America, be its glad ushers. Not by laying aside the distinctive character of our sex to enter the halls of legislation, as petitioners or otherwise,—not by banding into societies to debate and harangue on social evils and their redress—shall we win this high honor, but by ruling in the little realm of home, our legitimate domain, in the spirit of wisdom and of love, by cultivating every feminine grace and charm which may secure for us a wide social influence, and by using this influence to commend truth and holiness, to allay the animosities of party and the prejudices of caste, and to prove to the world that there is no civilization so high-toned and of such true refinement, as that which is based on Christian principles.

CHAPTER VIII.

THE WEST.

THE United States of America—how much is comprised in these few words! How many varieties of life, physical and spiritual! Here, forests seemingly interminable, where gigantic trees clothe themselves in the cheerful livery of spring, the full foliage of summer, the russet hues of autumn, or present their leafless branches to the tossings of the wintry tempests, with no human eye to mark their changes, no human voice to interrupt the harmony of their feathered songsters, and no human foot to startle the squirrel from his feast, or to track to his haunts the prowling wolf or savage bear;—there, cities, which from their artificial life and closely-pressed population, you might fancy coeval with the oldest of the old world. Here, a people who, cast upon rugged rocks, have become rugged as they, and forced from stern nature wealth and luxury, making the stones which she gave them for bread, build their houses, and compelling the streams which would not float their ships to turn their mill-wheels;—there, a land whose soil scarce needs the tillage of man to bring forth all that can charm the eye or gratify the appetite, yet whose inhabitants rarely obtain from it more than the necessaries of existence. Here, a territory whose dwellings stand ever clustered around the church and the school-house;—there, a vast extent of country over which no Sabbath bell has ever sounded, and where no schoolmaster has yet gone abroad. Yet, over this country, so diverse in its physical features and its moral aspect, there is still one bond of unity. All its citizens are politically free and independent; all profess to be, in some sense—though in what sense few of them perhaps understand—equal. To all of them, therefore, we may say, as we have said: "Your life must be moulded in other and simpler forms than that of lands whose civilization was the child of feudalism, not of Christianity."

But there are circumstances connected with these diversified modes of life, which must greatly modify the forms in each. Permit us to describe more minutely the variations to which each of these modes of life has already given rise, the evils to be dreaded in each, and, so far as our insight extends, the manner in which those evils may be avoided.

And first, of the West. Here we have a vast extent of territory, the first danger of whose inhabitants has been well defined by an able writer of our own land, to be barbarism, or a loss both of civilization and of Christianity. Nor can any doubt that there is sufficient cause for this fear, who casts an eye over this portion of our country, with its habitations scattered here and there at remote distances, and with no tie of mutual advantage holding together the dwellers in those habitations, or binding them to one common centre. In the most unmitigated form of this Western life, the single habitation of the rude squatter or adventurous hunter, ever receding before the advance of civilization, the evil is immedicable by any specific that we can command. But, here and there, over those pathless prairies, journeys a group of settlers, leaving the smiling homesteads where their childhood and youth have been passed in a life simple but not altogether rude, in search of richer if not happier fortunes in that far West which is the "land of promise" to the American of the Atlantic coast. These establish themselves on neighboring farms, in rude huts, in which they live perchance for years, estranged from all the customs and the comforts of their earlier life. No Sabbath bell reminds them that there is a higher nature within them to whose necessities one-seventh part of their time has been devoted by their great Law-giver; no ambassador from God, no messenger of the glad tidings of salvation, visits them in their comfortless abodes. Even the intellectual powers that fit them for the more successful pursuit of worldly objects, find there no means of cultivation—for no school-house rises within any convenient distance of their homes. The present, with its stern demands, which will brook no delay, presses away the memories of a former and happier life, and drowns by its clamors the still, small voice which would urge the claims of the future. They eat and drink and perish, with little but those fading memories to mark them as nobler than the brutes; and they leave their children to a life in which those memories have already assumed the less influential character of traditions.

Permit us to pause here for a moment with a suggestion which has often forced itself upon our hearts, while contemplating the condition of these our countrymen and countrywomen. It is this: how can any American seek his field of missionary labor in the distant isles of the

Pacific, in India, or China, or Africa, and leave thus, within the borders of his own land, a people speaking his own language, claiming a common parentage with himself, "bone of his bone and flesh of his flesh," to lose the light of the gospel, and sink back into darkness as deep as that of any Pagan land? True, from those distant parts of the earth voices are crying out to us in tones well nigh irresistible for the bread of life; nor would we resist the appeal—if we are Christians we dare not, for our work, if we are followers of Christ, is what his was, the salvation of the whole world. But while we do *this*, let us take heed that we leave not *the other* undone—that the neighbor at our door—the duty nearest us—be not overlooked! Ah! will not England and America learn, that to them, as to Israel of old, it is commanded, ere they go forth to do battle against the enemies of the Lord, and to overthrow the false gods of the Heathen, to "put away" from themselves "every wicked thing." Let us educate and Christianize our own people, that we may go forth with resistless power, even with the power of the Most High, to bring the whole earth into subjection to the truth which we have thus acknowledged and obeyed.

But this is a subject which may be thought somewhat

apart from our present design, and too high for our feeble pens; we turn, therefore, again to our own sex, and to the more common forms of life. And even here, in these western wilds, woman—and woman in the exercise only of her acknowledged powers, in the fulfilment of the sweet charities of home, as wife, mother, mistress—may do much to promote the advance of Christian civilization.

Not unfrequently the rude settlement formed by some band of Eastern emigrants, whose whole capital could do little more than purchase the land on which they built their huts, has been made in a spot possessing such advantages of position as to tempt others, with somewhat more capital, to plant their habitations near them. The unsuccessful merchant, and the professional man of expensive habits, who, having married early, finds his family increasing more rapidly than the means of supporting them in a land in which his class is already too numerous, look longingly to the West, where they may, without the humiliation of a descent in the social scale, assume a mode of life more simple and better suited to their reduced incomes. Too often, we grieve to say it, the consent of the wife to this removal is an enforced consent—and even where it is otherwise, where it is given from an intelligent conviction of the wisdom of such a measure, and a profound sympathy with the disappointments and the hopes of her husband, there is often, we fear, no consciousness of any duty on her part but endurance, cheerful as she can make it, of what she regards as the inevitable evils of her lot. Alas! she has yet to learn that, "to be still, sometimes demands immeasurably higher power than to act." It is only while we are actively engaged in efforts to meliorate suffering and to overcome evil, whether physical or moral, that we can cheerfully endure its presence. Let every Christian woman thus borne westward by influences over which she has no control, recognise in these influences the hand of Providence, and ask herself, What work has God here for me? and we shall have fewer instances of families driven back, through the discontent of the wife and mother, from the abodes which were just beginning to assume something of the aspect of homes, and from the property just beginning to repay the first expense of its settlement and the cares lavished upon it, wisely, but vainly. She comes—the unhappy wife—with her beauty faded by unaccustomed labor and privation, and the buoyancy of her spirit broken, and the serenity of her temper clouded by many cares; and the world, that wise judge, exclaims—"How cruel it is, to take a woman of refinement, who has been accustomed to all the comforts of civilized life, to the West!"

Sad sentence, this, if it be a true one, for it condemns that fair and fertile region, whose wide extent and rich resources give promise of power and wealth greater than those of all the rest of our confederacy, to the loss of those influences which will most successfully combat its present tendency to barbarism. While political economists are arguing on the danger to our institutions of the rapid increase of a foreign population in our land, and statesmen are planning checks and balances to this evil, the resistless flood is still rolling Westward—the roaring of its mighty wave breaking the silence of the prairies, over which for ages only the Indian moved with stealthy step, while the very winds seemed there to hush themselves to softer whisperings. There, Europe is pouring out her pent-up thousands. The overwrought children of toil from England and Scotland—the starving peasantry of Ireland, with their quick wit, and wild, reckless impulses—the Swiss, the German, the Dane, the Swede—all are there waiting the influences which are to fashion them into a terrible engine of destruction to a government which can rest securely only on the intelligence and virtue of its people, or to mould them into the choicest pillars of our Temple of Freedom. And shall we lightly reject in such a work the silent, but most powerful, influence of woman? Shall she, who might soften the rude, and tame the fierce, and harmonize the discordant elements of character, be forbidden to approach them? Rather let us rejoice to see our noblest and our best bending their steps thitherward, if they have minds to grasp the work that lies before them, physical powers to endure its demands, and hearts to give themselves to a noble cause in self-denying effort. All these will, we doubt not, be needed; therefore, let no woman, without counting the cost, consent to undertake this mission, for a sacred mission it must be to her. Before she enters on it, let her be assured that she has the true refinement which can sustain itself unharmed in the simplest life; an innate dignity which, dispensing with all the shows and trappings of a vain and selfish luxury, may still be intact in its essential grace. Fatigue she must doubtless endure, and therefore the need of physical vigor. To these attributes, she will require to add such a knowledge of all household economy, as shall make her not absolutely dependent upon hired services for the comforts of her home.

"Not dependent upon hired services! What! would you have a lady cook and wash?"—methinks we hear some astonished reader exclaim. Certainly not, we reply, if she can avoid it; but we would have her know how to perform even these offices if necessary; for we contend it is better to cook a dinner than to want one, and better, and more lady-like even, to wash our own clothing, than to wear it unclean. The last is a labor, however, which requires the strength of practised muscles, and might be found impossible to unaccustomed hands, were it not for the aid of those mechanical arts, to whose benign influence on social life we have already alluded.

Let us say to those who hear with scorn of *ladies* so engaged, that we have known, even here, the fair daughter of luxury who had been delicately reared, in anticipation of a life that should be as a fairy dream, suddenly driven from her home of affluence to one of poverty; and never did we so value the accomplishments which were intended to give a new charm to the promise of her earlier days, as when we saw them cheering and brightening, not herself only, but all who dwelt within the shadow of her darkened life. Never have we found beauty so alluring or grace so winning, as when we have seen them employed in the homeliest labors, and learned thus how much they might do to win for labor the respect which is its due, and to elevate the laborer even in his own esteem. Yet, we may add, there would probably be less necessity for the performance of these labors, in their Western homes, by those to whom they are an untried and therefore a formidable exertion, if they would seek the aid of their neighbors in the wilderness, in the spirit of those who ask an interchange of kindly offices from their equals, rather than of those who purchase the services of their inferiors. Remember, that the unlettered woman to whom you apply yourself with such an air of hauteur, has yet to learn the value of that cultivation on which you found your claim to superiority—that of the accomplishments which are your boast she knows nothing, while she sees you ignorant of those arts which are of prime necessity in your present life—the only life with which she is acquainted. Can you wonder that she is slow to perceive and acknowledge herself your inferior? Nay, the fact of superiority or inferiority may bear a debate from whatever point we take our view, while we look only at the relative accomplishments and acquirements of the two parties. Yours we admire most, perhaps, but we can live without them; hers are of prime necessity. The true superiority of yours consists in their power to enlarge the boundaries of thought and feeling —to give you sources of happiness elevated above all the accidents of your present condition. If they have done this for you, your superiority will soon assert itself, and be acknowledged without any trouble on your part. The cultivation which gives you command of temper under all the trials of your life, the accomplishments which communicate somewhat of grace and elegance to your rude home, and which make you courteous and kindly to the untutored beings around you, cannot fail in time to win their respect, and even to inspire them with the desire to emulate in some degree what they admire. We can scarcely hope, indeed, to excite this latter feeling in the breasts of those who have grown old in such different habits. But the sapling may yield to the force which will not suffice to bend the stalwart oak. The young will be there, whose quick affections and eager faculties are so quickly won to love, admire, and imitate; and when you have thus influenced them, how noble will be your work—how great your reward! The brightening aspect of the homes around you, the purer tastes and gentler manners of the dwellers in those homes will be as a perpetual blessing to you. Do you ask any other reward? You will find it in the increased value of your own home—in the conviction that you may dwell in it without fear of coarse and brutalizing associations for your children—that by interesting them in your own holy work, you may even find there more fully than in more advanced societies the proper stimulus for all in them which is "pure and lovely and of good report." And with these "dearer and home-felt delights" may mingle the sweet thought, that silently, unseen, like the rill which steals along, marking its course only by the verdure to which it supplies a richer green and more luxuriant beauty, you have done more real good to your country, more to insure the continuance of institutions depending on the intelligence and virtue of her people, than all the demagogues who ever harangued in or out of Congress.

CHAPTER IX.

THE SOUTH.

The South! the sunny South! The land where the snow-spirit never comes, where the forest-trees are never stripped of their green coronal, where Spring flings her flowers into the very lap of Winter! Let us stand beneath her soft skies, inhale the perfume of her myrtle-bowers and orange-groves, press her violet-covered turf, and weave fragrant wreaths of the jessamine which flings its yellow clusters so gracefully from tree to tree. Or, if you would look on nature in a soberer dress, we will walk through her forests of pine, and listen to the whispering of the winds as they pass over them; or we will stand beneath the giant oaks, from whose branches a gray, mossy drapery hangs waving in the summer breeze, while the ocean wave breaks with a lulling murmur at our feet. To eyes accustomed to bolder views—to precipitous rocks and lofty mountains, and all the pleasing variety of hill and dale—these beauties may seem tame, yet no true lover of nature can look long without some melting of the heart, upon that rich and varied foliage, that flowery earth, and those ever sparkling, ever dancing waters. Theirs is not the beauty which strikes with sudden, overpowering admiration, but they steal not less surely to the heart; and when, bruised and worn with the conflicts of life, we shrink from great emotions and long only for repose, the memory of their peaceful loveliness comes back on our spirits, with an influence soothing as that of the mother's smile which lulled our infancy to rest.

It will be evident to those acquainted with the physical features of our country, that we have been describing only the Atlantic coast of the Southern States; for as we advance into the interior, the face of the country becomes more broken, and rises to greater elevation, until, at the distance of less than one hundred miles from the sea, the Alleghany rears its lofty summits. A noble country is this interior—its aspect wild and picturesque, its soil fertile, and its mineral wealth unbounded; but it is yet, like the West, in that state of transition which offers few distinctive features to the observers of moral and social life. New settlers are still migrating thither from the North and East, bearing with them the impressions and habits of their former homes; and it will probably be long before they are welded together in one homogeneous mass. But on the Southern seacoast, we have a social life which has existed nearly as long as any in our land, and which is marked by peculiar characteristics, the result of peculiar institutions.

In sketching the circumstances under which the earliest settlements in these United States were made, we did not allude to one element introduced into Southern life, and Southern life alone. It is one, in truth, which we would fain have avoided altogether, for its very name has been of late years a signal for strife. But to write of the South and say nothing of slave-labor, were indeed —to borrow the words of John Randolph, on another subject—" to give the tragedy of Hamlet, with the part of Hamlet omitted;" for from this domestic institution does the South derive many of those traits which have given her a distinctive character, and assigned to her a distinctive part in the great drama acting in this land. We have seen that in every part of our country the prosperity of the colonists began only when they threw off their dependence on their foreign patrons; but ere this had been done, those patrons had, in some instances, accomplished plans whose influence, for good or for evil, is still felt by us. Such was the act introducing African laborers, as slaves, into the Southern colonies. Vainly did the colonists protest against this act—vainly seek its annulment by the Board of Directors in England. Wise men were those who formed that board! Did the future unroll itself before their wondering eyes? Did they see, far down the tide of time, those feeble colonies become a great nation, no longer bringing tribute to England, or accepting laws from her; and did a mocking laugh rise to their lips as they heard their own sons—the sons of those by whose command, if not by whose very hands, the African was brought to America, and condemned to his life-bondage—the sons of those either in England or in New England who received all the gain of this infamous traffic, branding as men-stealers the children of the very men now petitioning to be delivered from the incubus of slavery? Strange things must the angels see in this our world! But we are nearing the abyss of strife—we feel its hot fires burning on our brow and kindling a flame in our heart, and we gladly turn from the acts of men, inconsistent, vacillating, and unjust, to those of the all-perfect One, "with whom is no variableness nor shadow of turning;" and we think it will not be difficult to prove from the annals of African slavery in this land, that He has made the wrath of man to praise Him—transmuting, with heavenly alchemy, the loathsome selfishness and heartlessness of the slave-trader into the partial civilization and Christianization of the race enslaved, and into the means of promoting the intellectual culture and social refinement of those who were forced into the position of their masters.

The improvement of the African race among us is sufficiently attested by the contrast which even the slaves in our Southern States present, to the specimens of the same race occasionally recaptured from some slave-ship and brought to our shores, some forty or fifty years ago. And now, yearly, many of this oppressed and much-wronged people are returning to their own land, bearing with them the seeds of all that has made us what we are. They went forth weeping, and they return bearing precious sheaves. The foul spirits which haunted the shores of Africa have been exorcised; Christian temples are rising there, and around those temples are clustered the habitations of civilized men, from which the voice of prayer and praise ascends to Heaven like the evening and the morning incense.

In proof of our second proposition, that the introduction of slavery into the United States had been made to subserve the promotion of intellectual culture and social refinement among ourselves, we will refer the reader to a work by one who cannot be suspected of favoring slavery —Dr. Bushnell, of Hartford. The argument to which we allude is contained in a sermon, published by him some months since, entitled, "Barbarism our first danger." He there asserts that, in colonization, the colony must always retrograde from the civilization of the parent-land, since little time can be spared for the refinements of life, by those who are engaged in a hand-to-hand contest with nature for the indispensable requisites of existence. From the action of this law, however, he confesses that those colonies in our land into which slave-labor was introduced, were comparatively free. There, the owner of property, having his land tilled by other hands, had leisure for the cultivation of his mind, and the practice of all the gentle courtesies of life. His gains, too, were immediate, and he was thus able to command the means of sending his sons to England for their education, while the youth of other portions of our land were educated at native schools and by native teachers. Was not the great prominence of our Southern statesmen, in the earlier years of our republic, the result of the superiority in the education which they thus received? This, her glorious crown, has fallen from the head of the South, and the sceptre is fast passing from her hands. Since they could not send their sons abroad for education, the Northern colonists struggled nobly and successfully to establish within their own borders the institutions necessary to mental culture. The result was another proof that in self-dependence lies self-reliance, self-help; for it has been hither, to this rude, laborious North, that Southern youth have come to receive an education, for the last fifty years.

We have presented these results of African slavery in our land, not to excuse the wrong-doing of men, by whom they could not have been foreseen, and of whose motives they could therefore have formed no part, but as evidence of the infinite wisdom and goodness of the world's Ruler. May we not be encouraged by such evidence to believe that He will yet bring good, *all good*, out of this evil? With hearts strengthened by such a faith, we may return to that fair Southern land, whose physical features we attempted to portray at the commencement of this chapter;—we will enter her habitations, and hold converse with her children—we will mark her social life, and see what woman has done there, and what yet remains for her to do. In fulfilling this design, it is not necessary that we should enter into the moral question involved in the existence of slavery; for we write not for men, who make and may therefore unmake the laws, but for women, whose benevolence and charity should be a law unto themselves, softening the pressure of the fetters which they cannot break, and lightening the darkness which they may not wholly dispel.

At the first glance which we give to Southern life, we perceive one point of striking contrast to life in the Northern and Middle States. The latter are chiefly commercial, and in them wealth, talent, and energy, are concentrated in cities. The former is agricultural, and there towns are few and small. The largest towns increase slowly, and some that were built a century ago have been deserted, their inhabitants having retired to their plantations. Nor could this well be avoided, for he who continues in the relation of a master cannot absolve himself from its obligations, and those obligations cannot be fulfilled in continual absence from the dependants for whose interests, temporal and eternal, he is bound "to watch as one that must give account." Especially should the gentle care of woman not be withdrawn from the home of the slave. She should be there to interpose the shield of her charity between the weak and the strong, to watch beside the sick, to soothe the sorrowing, to teach the ignorant, to soften by her influence the haughty master, and to elevate the debased slave. We know that there are women—women in the often misrepresented South, who have lived and do live for such objects. They will have their reward; their names may be cast out as evil in the world, but "they shall be found written in the Lamb's book of life." Such should be the life of every Southern woman. She is a missionary to whose own door God has brought the Pagans to be instructed. Ah! could she but understand all her mission, could she possess her soul in patience in the midst of the warring elements which surround her—could she pour the oil of her own loving and gentle thoughts upon the raging waters of strife, winning the fiery natures around her to see the good even in their enemies, to adopt wise counsel even though it come mingled with bitter taunt, to foster the rare magnanimity which will not be withheld from a right action by the apprehension that a foe may regard it as a concession—could she induce, or even strive to induce them to do all this—exercising her influence, not by public associations, and debates, and petitions, but in the manifestation of all feminine grace, and all womanly delicacy—she would prove herself indeed, what one of old named her, the connecting link between man and the angelic world.

On Southern plantations the houses are generally of wood, large and commodious, but built with little regard to elegance, and furnished with a simplicity which would shock the eye of a third-rate votary of fashion in a Northern city. In these simple homes, however, you may enter without fear; "stranger" is there a sacred name; and you will find youself entertained with an open-hearted hospitality which may well reconcile you to the absence of some accustomed luxuries. In the dwellers in these homes, you will find generally the easy, courteous bearing which distinguishes the best society everywhere. In them, too, you will often find the highest intelligence in the land; and it will be readily perceived, that the result of this attainment of high cultivation in the inartificial life of the country, must be the formation of a character uniting, in a rare degree, refinement and simplicity. To this union, we think, Southern women are indebted for that charm so generally attributed to their manner—a charm which is never felt so fully as in their own homes, where all around them wears the impress of their own spirits. In the life they lead, there is little of moment but personal qualities. The fact that the changes of property are less frequent and violent in an agricultural than in a commercial country—that families remain longer in their relative positions in the first than in the last—has given, it is true, a higher value to blood,—to family distinction,—at the South than at the North, yet scarcely sufficient to affect the reception of an individual in society. The true gold of character will there pass current, even though it may lack "the guinea stamp."

Yet, even in this life, simple, unostentatious as it is, we find some vestiges of the old feudalism. One of these vestiges we recognise in the universal contempt for labor—not perhaps in itself considered, but as pursued for gain. A GENTLEMAN may labor, he may be his own blacksmith or carpenter, if such be his taste, but he must make it evident that it is his taste—that he has no ulterior design to profit by his labors—if he would not lose caste. Were this prejudice entertained only against such rude employments as we have named, however, we could scarcely represent it as characteristic of the South. The hard-handed mechanic, however intelligent and even polite, is as completely shut out from the pale of good society everywhere; but at the South, even the merchant finds himself somewhat slightly regarded, because engaged in a money-getting occupation. This has doubtless been the result of that severance of the natural connection between property and labor which has obtained at the South, and in which lies the very essence of feudalism. Through this, the association of *otium cum dignitate* was established and has been perpetuated at the South. Through this, the military profession has been honored there, even as in European countries in old feudal times. Next in dignity stands the legal profession, the great nursery of statesmen in our land; then the clerical and medical professions; while the life of elegant leisure which the resources of a few enable them to lead, is regarded as equal or superior to any of these in the social position it confers.

In the Northern and Middle States, an idle man seems in an awkward position, as the world of his acquaintance is hurrying by him; he must assume a bustling manner, that he may, at least, *seem* to be employed. At the South, he stands in an attitude of graceful repose, and looks with conscious superiority upon the workers around him. But this state of things cannot endure. Every day, and in every place, the conviction is becoming more decided, that this is a working world. There is work here for each and all, and he who does not his own share, makes his brother's burden by so much the heavier. Work! though it be only to improve your own land; and if you work successfully, the world has become so much richer by your labors. Especially in a country professedly republican, can no wise or conscientious man remain an idler. Do you really value your country, her freedom, her intelligence? Awake, sluggard! lift up your eyes, and see how the darkness from other lands is overshadowing her intelligence—how the oppressed multitudes of other nations, escaping from their galling bonds, threaten, in their wild transports, to trample freedom under foot, and to introduce in her place the anarchy which has ever ended, and must ever end in despotism. Here are the ignorant to be taught, the weak to be guided, the vicious to be reclaimed. Up, then, and be doing!—while a school or a church is needed in the remotest district, you have something for which to labor. We feel persuaded that even in the South, the listless repose of the idle will not long continue undisturbed. Changes have already taken place there which betoken the infusion of new elements into its indolent *poco-curante* life. These elements are, we believe, the overflowing of the ever-boiling and bubbling caldron of life in the New England and Middle States. A happy admixture will this be, if the South will receive strength and activity, and give refinement, without suffering simplicity to be lost in the exchange.

Changes, we repeat, have already taken place at the South. Manufactories have been erected there, mines have been worked, and railroads opened, in almost every available direction. Should the prejudice against labor continue in its full force at the South, these newly-opened sources of wealth must fall into the hands of the strangers who first found the key to them, and the old proprietors be overshadowed till they die out of the soil which gave them birth. But of this we have little fear. We do not think that any part of our country can much longer remain unenlightened on the beneficence, the true nobleness of labor, nay, of labor for money, since in money lies the germ of all the good we may do, as well as of that we may enjoy. We will suppose all error on this subject to have been rectified, and Southern society to have become an industrious, active, energetic, money-getting society. Then arises another, and, to us, not less interesting question. Will it, in acquiring the virtues of the North, retain its own? Will its members, while adding to their homes the mechanical improvements which minister to comfort, and the treasures of art which at once form and gratify the taste—while thus gaining all that is truly valuable in the most advanced civilization, still wisely refuse to exchange their simple, social habits for the ostentatious display and vulgar pretension which too often mark a sudden increase of wealth? If they do, if maintaining their simplicity of life, they awake to a sense of their responsibility to God and to the world for the improvement and proper use of every talent entrusted to them, if they become "*workers* with God," seeking wealth,

> "Not for to hide it in a hedge,
> Nor for a train attendant—
> But for the glorious privilege"

of opening to others a nobler life, of elevating to the dignity of men their own dependants, of sending the purifying streams of Christian education through the land—that, each man learning he is the brother of all, the bitter prejudices of sect and party may be discarded, and our country, our whole country, become what God intended it to be, united in one spirit, as well as in one body: if they do all this, then will they have attained to our conception of a true American life.

And has woman at the South nothing to do in promoting this "consummation most devoutly to be wished?" It must be mainly her work. Let her place it before her as an object of her life. Let her improve every gift and cultivate every grace, that the increased influence thus obtained may aid in its accomplishment. Let her light so shine that it may enlighten all who come within her sphere. Let her be a teacher of the ignorant, a guide to the straying of her own household. Let her make it a law of the social life in which she rules, that nothing so surely degrades a man as idleness, and the vices to which it almost inevitably leads. Thus will she proclaim the dignity and worth of labor, and she will find her reward in the new impress made on the yet ductile minds of her children. She has seen them hitherto too often go forth like bright but wandering stars, into a life containing for them no definite object. In this vast void, she has seen them too often driven hither and thither by their own reckless impulses; and her heart has been wrung, and her imploring cry has arisen to Heaven for God's restraining grace, as they have seemed about to rush into the unfathomable realm of night. With almost Spartan heroism she has offered her "Te Deums," as again and again the sound has come up to her from the battle-field of life—"Mother! all is lost, but honor!" But labor will tame these wild impulses—will give to life a decided aim; and, as the strong hand, loosed from the bonds of prejudice, obeys the command of the stout heart, her "pæans" will be sounded, not for defeat nobly sustained, but for victory won. We have placed before her, her work and her reward.

CHAPTER X.

THE NORTH-EASTERN AND MIDDLE STATES.

From the boundless prairie and the pathless forest of the West, with all their sublime associations, their touching reminiscences of an empire past, their grand promise of a nobler empire yet to come;—from the South, with its quiet loveliness of broad rivers, flowing with gentle, noiseless current through valleys clothed with all the exuberance of vegetation common to those lands which lie nearest the sun;—from the rude strength of the one and the refined simplicity of the other,—from these pictures of life so different, and each so complete in itself, we turn to the North and East, and for a time all before us seems a great kaleidoscope of ever-shifting forms and colors, without plan or definite arrangement. Bustling crowds are moving hither and thither across the area of our vision, jostling and even trampling each other; but by what spirit are they impelled?—what object are they pursuing?—to what bourne are they speeding?

The rapid variations of fortune resulting from commercial enterprise, have a tendency to engender feverish dreams and wild speculations. Life, under such circumstances, becomes a great game of chance. Men move through its shifting scenes with knitted brows, and throbbing pulses, and anxious hearts, like those who feel that the next throw of the dice, or turn of the wheel of fortune may place them at the summit on which all eyes are fastened, and to which all efforts are straining, or may cast them down to the very foot of that eminence up which they have been toiling for weary years. And it is by this spirit—the anxious, self-absorbed spirit of the gamester—that the movements of most men here are impelled. We say, of *most* men, for we believe there are few comparatively who hold themselves aloof from mercantile speculation in some of its forms. The lawyer, the physician, and even the divine, if we mistake not, has often the product of years of labor placed, not where, guarded with unquestionable security, it may bring to him a moderate interest, but in some popular stock, or surprisingly lucrative business, where, at some acknowledged hazard, it promises to double, or treble, or quadruple itself in an incredibly short time.

And what is the object pursued with such ardor? Is

it gold alone? Are these men indeed so sordid that they are willing to bury all the nobler parts of their nature in shining dust? No; gold is not their ultimate object. Gold is but the representative of that distinction which man everywhere craves, and which under our present social arrangements can be obtained ordinarily only through wealth.

The tone of feeling which prevails in the New England and Middle states, in regard to labor, seems more decidedly American than we have found it elsewhere. The idler is viewed with little respect. Each man has, or seeks to have, a work to do—at least the exceptions to this remark are so few, that they serve, by the observation they excite, to prove the rule. Yet it is here that the influence of the old feudal life is most powerfully manifested—here that the most slavish subjection to European customs is found. "You talk of despotism abroad," said an intelligent foreigner to a friend, after a residence of a few months in this part of our country; "there is no despotism like that of fashion in America." Having adopted foreign lawgivers, we seem to have retained no discretionary power over their edicts. Did this affect only our outer life—the form of our dresses and our furniture, our style of architecture and our carriages—we should say nothing, unless indeed we adverted to it to express our thanks to those who, by the exercise of their powers on these necessary yet not very important arrangements of social life, had left ours free for other and higher objects. But this is not all. Not a folly, or even a vice, is tolerated abroad, in what are called the higher circles, but it finds apologists and imitators here. He who has spent years enough abroad to divest himself of all that was American about him—who returns hither only because his exhausted finances will not support his extravagances in other lands—becomes at once "the glass of fashion and the mould of form." Our good plain English, the language suiting men of sound practical minds and true feeling, is exchanged for a jargon of various tongues, and American wives and daughters grow ashamed in his presence, of their power to make home comfortable as well as gay, ashamed of all which makes their true glory and excellence. The result of this is often a compromise, awkward and inharmonious as compromises ordinarily are, between the American characteristics early acquired, and the foreign graces grafted upon them. It cannot, we hope, be supposed for a moment, that we are so illiberal, so ignorant, and unjust, as to stigmatize all which is foreign as evil. There is one even now amongst us, who has taught us that home, with its cares and its joys, is in Sweden, as in America, the sanctuary of true and warm affections, the nursery of pure and high thoughts. But let it be remembered that we do not obtain the better aspects of social life abroad—not the home-life—from the sources to which we have alluded—and while there is not a nation in Europe from which we would not gladly receive lessons—not one which we would not be proud to resemble in some of its characteristics—we would still preserve an independent mind, free to try all, to judge all, and to hold fast only that which is good. We would take an intelligent view of our own position, and of the objects for which we exist as a separate people, and we would adopt nothing which would unfit us for that position, or shackle us in the attainment of those objects.

We have been accustomed to speak of that nation as having attained to the highest civilization, in which the greatest advance had been made in the cultivation of and provision for the physical nature, though the advantages thus gained were enjoyed only by a few. But this is a civilization to which a Pagan land might equally have attained; it is not the civilization to which a nation whose corner-stone was laid on the basis of a pure Christian faith should aspire. Let it be our boast, that we have placed the spiritual above the physical—that though our houses may want some conveniences and luxuries common abroad, though our theatres and our operas may be less magnificent than those of other lands—our schools and our churches are more numerous and better supported. Let us acknowledge that the outward graces of life, and what we are accustomed to term the accomplishments of education, are found in higher perfection with a fortunate few abroad, than with us. We may willingly consent to postpone any effort to compete with their possessors, while we are engaged in the nobler task of educating the spiritual natures of all the dwellers in our land—of pouring light on the benighted minds, and clothing with "the beauty of holiness" the debased spirits sent to us from countries boasting, and boasting justly, their higher civilization. We do not undervalue this civilization. We are not blind to the grace of form or the splendor of coloring, or deaf to the charms of music, or insensible to the thousand luxuries it has introduced. We rejoice to see some in our own land achieve for themselves by successful industry, the power of commanding these luxuries. We look with pleasure, nay, with somewhat of honest pride on the success of our countrymen, on the stately dwellings rising around us. We mark with satisfaction the improvements in architectural taste, and the advances in all that may minister to comfort. Especially do we take delight in finding in these dwellings objects for the gratification of the higher tastes, the creations of the chisel and the pencil, lifting us into communion with the artist in his moments of inspiration, and those silent counsellors, books, in which are treasured the wisdom of ages. No cloud dims our satisfaction in the observation of these acquisitions, till we see that their possessor regards them as having transmuted his common clay into the fine porcelain of earth, —that, from the height to which he has attained, he looks down on those struggling, even as he did but a few short years ago, not to cheer them by his example, not to extend to them a helping hand, but to depress them by his insolent assumption, and to provoke them to an unwise and ruinous expenditure in the assertion of that equality which he is so ready to deny. It is to this last influence of the arrogant spirit which sudden elevation awakens in a vulgar mind, that we owe our most urgent social evils. From this it proceeds that almost all in our large cities live, if not beyond, at least to the utmost extent of their incomes. To this we may trace the anxious faces we meet ever and again in our walks; to this, the fretful tempers which have driven peace from the once happy family; to this, the ruined health of women whose cheerful smiles once made the sunlight of their homes. We do not mean that this influence is evident to the consciousness of each who thus suffers from it. Many of these sufferers would, we doubt not, indignantly deny its control over their actions. They will tell you they but do what is common for others in their circumstances; they ask not what gave the impetus to those who began this fearful race—this dance of death, as it has proved to so many. But will not their secret hearts bear witness, that they do submit to much wearing anxiety, and even to great sacrifices of personal comfort, which they might avoid if they were willing to occupy less spacious apartments, to tread on carpets of more homely texture, and to sit at tables where the equally bounteous, perhaps the more bounteous meal, was served in less costly dishes?

Permit us, in illustration of this subject, to present a sketch of what is happening every day in our midst. A young man—nay, we beg pardon, a young *gentleman*—who has been accustomed by the habits and the language of his home, to consider a certain style of living essential to the maintenance of his social position, marries one whose serene, joyous temper gives him assurance of a happy home. Love would fain build a palace costly as Aladdin's for the loved one, but as love has no credit in the market, he is compelled to be limited in his arrangements by the amount of money he can pay or promise. At least, however, he will do the utmost that he honestly may to make her home worthy of her. He looks around among his acquaintances possessing about the same amount of wealth as himself for a model on which to form his *ménage,* and in accordance with prevailing custom, a house much larger than they need is bought, or hired, and furnished with at least as much regard to show as comfort. His task completed, he looks upon its result with pride as well as pleasure, and reflects with complacency, that as two persons will want but little attendance, and no great outlay in the supply of the table, any deficit occasioned by this first great draft upon their fortune, will soon be replaced. Under these impressions their married life begins joyfully. The young wife soon finds, however, that the mistress of a large house and splendid furniture, with few servants, has no sinecure place. Her servants, to whom she had perhaps dreamed of being a friend and guide, whom she had perhaps once regarded as having a right to some little time for the consideration of higher objects than cooking and washing, sweeping and dusting, become in her eyes only useful machines, valued according to the rapidity and accuracy with which they perform their labors. But these machines are human. They become exhausted by labor, and the smiling, ready, cheerful service is exchanged for sullen looks and movements. Then we hear, "—— has stayed long enough with us, she is spoiled;" and the first expression of dissatisfaction in the poor wearied girl, is eagerly seized as a pretext for dismissing her and supplying her place with another machine whose unworn springs may work more briskly. But this is not the limit of the evil. An increasing family brings increased expenditure, while the fortune remains unchanged. Retrenchment must be made where the world will least perceive it. A servant, perhaps, is dismissed, and the wife must supply by her increased labor the place thus vacated. Farewell now to the cultivation of taste, the improvement of intellect, which had been connected in her dreams with her married life. Work—work—work, till heart and hand fail, till the cloud gather on her once sunny brow, and her cheeks grow pale, and friendly consumption come to give her rest from her labors in the grave, or the throbbing brain and over-anxious heart overpower the reason, and a lunatic asylum receive one more miserable inmate. Think not this is an exaggerated picture, or the last an unusual destination under such circumstances. In a report of the officers for the Retreat of the Insane, in Hartford, Connecticut, which lies before us, the intelligent and humane superintendent and physician, Dr. Butler, says: "In many cases, not having received in early life a judicious physical or moral training for her new and arduous station, the young wife, impelled by affection and an honest pride to her utmost efforts, soon finds that, with her increasing family, the burden of care and duties increases; while her physical strength and capacity of endurance diminish even in a greater ratio. An economy sometimes deemed necessary, more often ill-judged and cruel, leads the husband to refrain from supplying the necessary domestic assistance; the nurse is discharged too soon, and sometimes no suitable one is provided. . . . . Thus it must naturally follow, that, between child-bearing, nursing, and the accumulation of household duties and drudgery, the poor heart-broken and disappointed wife loses, in turn, her appetite, her rest, and her strength; her nervous system is prostrated, and sinking under her burden, she seeks refuge in a lunatic hospital. *This process of inducing insanity is by no means limited to the above-mentioned classes; the same thing, differing more in degree than in manner, is often seen elsewhere.*"

Now let us see what might have been the destiny of this same woman. Suppose that some good angel had whispered to the young lover—"Ye, who are a world to each other, need not care for the world's opinion of your home." Imagine him, then, selecting for their future abode a house convenient and comfortable, rather than large or showy. Good taste is combined with economy in its furniture. If in any thing he is tempted to overstep his prescribed limits, it is not in those rooms that are to meet the curious eyes of the indifferent, but in that innermost shrine of the sanctuary of his home, to which only the dearly loved shall be admitted. He may indulge himself in adorning the walls of this room with an exquisite painting, or in placing in it some article of graceful luxury. For this simple home he will have abundant attendance. In this outlay he rejects all the whispered cautions of economy, aye, even though they come to his ear from the voice he best loves. "Not a cent," he says, "for show, but every thing for comfort" —and what comfort so dear to him as to secure the companionship of her he loves—to have her meet him with unexhausted powers—to give her the leisure necessary for the continued improvement of her mind, and for the preservation of her youth in its fresh, joyous spring?

And she, whose faculties have thus found a congenial soil—shall she idly enjoy the gifts of Heaven? She will not, if she be worthy of the home we have endeavored to describe. Of that home she is to be the presiding genius. From her its spirit will be caught. She cannot make it an Eden, for its flowers will wither. Sickness and sorrow and death will enter it; but in the warmth and light reflected on it from the sunshine of her soul, shall grow all pure and gentle affections—no rivalry, no vain ambition can live there. There no hurrying step and anxious look shall excite in the mind of a visiter distrust of his welcome; but in the aspect of all around him he shall read the salutation—"Peace be unto you!" While refusing to waste her strength, sour her temper, and burden her domestics, in a vain effort to *seem* to live as those do who can command an income twice as large as her own, she will, by a wise economy, make her resources available for the largest possible amount of comfort for all the inmates of her home. Nor will she be unmindful of beauty in its arrangements. It is her bower of love, and, as such, she will delight to decorate it by her pure taste. Yet all outward adornments shall be subservient to spiritual beauty. No costly luxury or treasure of art shall be purchased by her with the pence wrung from the honest wages of laborious poverty. The contentment that sits upon her husband's brow, the joyous faces of her children, the smiling, grateful countenances of her servants, the esteem of the friends who love to partake the serene enjoyments of her fireside, the blessings of the poor to whom her benevolence is extended—these are her luxuries, these the treasures she covets.

Such a home is a temple from which anthems of praise are continually ascending to the Most High. And is it a Utopian dream, that such may be the prevailing character of American homes? It is a dream which must become a reality, when our social life shall be modelled on the principles we have endeavored to unfold in this little volume. There are few, comparatively, in our land who may not hope by industry, sobriety, and economy, to obtain an income sufficient to lift them above sordid poverty—few who may not receive a good school education—few who, if they will relinquish all desire for a display disproportioned to their means, may not command the comforts of life by their labor, and yet reserve some time for spiritual cultivation. But while the wife and daughters of him who but yesterday plodded with weary step and anxious heart through our places of business, look down to-day from their gilded saloons with haughty coldness upon those who have been less fortunate in the race of life—and while the first, whatever may be their ignorance, inanity, or vulgarity, are received in society with a distinction which the last, whatever be their personal qualities, would vainly claim, there will be few so self-sustained, few so truly noble, as to relinquish all social consideration, rather than debase themselves by a contest in which success can be gained only by a loss of integrity, of self-respect, and of peace.

On the women of the United States, especially on those of the Middle and Eastern States, dwelling in cities where all the varied forms of life are brought closely in contact, does it chiefly, if not wholly depend, whether our country is to assume a social attitude in harmony with her political pretensions; whether our civilization is to be of a nobler sort than any the world has yet known, a civilization founded on the brotherhood of man, in which the poorest laborer shall be recognised as an heir of immortality, a child of God, and as such shall have room for the growth of his spiritual faculties, and be respected according to the advancement of those faculties; or whether ours shall be a vain attempt to cope with the civilization of feudal lands, in the gorgeous displays by which they strike the senses and win the homage of the uncultivated. In choosing the first of these forms of development, we ask you to relinquish no luxury, to sacrifice no enjoyment, which your resources can command without pressing on your brother man. Build palaces, if you can—fill them with all that can charm the eye, delight the ear, or gratify sinlessly any sense; but forget not that you are stewards of God, that you are surrounded by your brethren, that you have been brought, by a wise Providence, to a point of time and space when and where you may act most easily and efficiently in accordance with the great principles of our Christian faith, principles reiterated in our national creed. Remember that no display is consistent with true nobility—we will leave out of the question the higher motive of Christian principle—which compels you to be a hard task-mistress to others; which forbids you to make such a remuneration for their labor as you feel in your heart it deserves; or which obliges you to claim from them for that which you do give, such entire devotion of their time and faculties as will leave them no hope of future advancement, no possibility of spiritual cultivation. If you have been placed upon an eminence, let the reflection that you cannot, like some of other lands, claim an indefeasible and divine right to your position, make you considerate of those who are toiling painfully towards you; and let them not find, when they have elevated themselves to your level, that you have so walled yourselves in that they may not stand by your side.

Our fathers, captivated by the beautiful ideal of a spiritual freedom incompatible with the old forms of life, followed, as we have seen, the angel of their vision across unknown seas, to the untrodden wilderness of a new world. To them the rudest hut on which that beatific presence rested was a nobler and a prouder dwelling than the palace of a king. What was to them the coarse garb, the scanty food, the rude shelter, for which they had exchanged a life of luxury, if they won in the exchange the right to "call no man master on earth," and to give the intelligent and joyful worship of free souls to "Him who was their master in Heaven?" And have we, their daughters, nothing akin in our natures to these lofty spirits? Shall we woo back to the fair homes which they bequeathed us a despotism sterner than that from which they fled? Shall we place the idols of earthly pomp and power on the pure shrines which they devoted to the spirit of universal freedom? Say not that theirs were the feelings and the work of men. Women delicately reared—women nurtured in the peaceful and luxurious homes of England, accompanied them hither. To these women posterity has raised no monument, history recorded no eulogium; yet when we think of them as pursuing, within their forest homes, their gentle, household tasks, sometimes, it may be, waking the silent echoes with their hymns of lofty cheer—even while in every whisper of the winds they must have dreamed of the Indian's stealthy step, in every sudden call fancied his cry of death—they seem to us not less heroic than those who, buckling on their armor, went forth to do battle with their savage foe; nay, were not theirs among those circumstances in which, "to be still, demands immeasurably higher power than to act?"

What, think you, was the American life, in their understanding of its import? Was it a life of unsubstantial forms—a life of selfish, individual aggrandizement? Rather, was it not a life of earnest purpose, of noble aim—a life of self-sacrifice for the assertion of great principles, with which the advancement of the human race was indissolubly connected? Such we believe it was, and such would we have ours to be. We would, like them, place before us a noble ideal, and go steadily forward to its attainment, even though it demanded the sacrifice of all which the world is accustomed to value most. And we would resemble them, not only in the object sought, but in their manner of seeking it. They claimed no place in council-halls or amid embattled hosts —"their voices were not heard in the street." Their power was in the example of their cheerful endurance, and in the silent influences of the homes over which they ruled. In those homes, men breathed an atmosphere which gave strength to every lofty impulse, and decision to every noble aim. From such homes men might come forth hard and stern, with too little of the spirit of Him who wept over the unbelief of the Jews, and refused to pronounce sentence of condemnation against a guilty woman; but in them, they sacrificed to no little vanity, frittered away their powers in no sensual pursuits. Without were strife, and danger, and bloodshed—all that make men hard; but within were purity and peace —the peace which ever dwells with those who live for the performance of duty.

There are some, perhaps, who will say—"This is all

true; but it is only great occasions that give opportunity for the exhibition of great qualities. Those of whom you speak have fought the battle and won the victory; nothing remains for us, but to enjoy the fruits of their labors."

And is it indeed so? Look abroad—see how the oppressed of other lands are fleeing hither, as to a city of refuge. Ignorance, and error, and superstition, follow fast in their rear. Is there, in such circumstances, no opportunity for the exhibition of great qualities, for self-denying generosity, for patient endurance, for courageous action in the great cause of human happiness? Will you object that these, the natives of another land, have no claim on you for the exercise of such qualities? Carlyle, in his own quaint, yet powerful style, tells an anecdote which may give a sufficient answer to such an objection. Here it is: "A poor Irish widow, her husband having died in one of the lanes of Edinburgh, went forth, with her three children, bare of all resource, to solicit help from the charitable establishments of that city. At this charitable establishment and then at that she was refused, referred from one to the other, helped by none, till she had exhausted them all; till her strength and heart failed her: she sank down in typhus fever, died, and infected her lane with fever, so that seventeen other persons died of fever there in consequence. The humane physician asks, thereupon, as with a heart too full for speaking—Would it not have been economy to help this poor widow? She took typhus fever, and killed seventeen of you! Very curious. The forlorn Irish widow applies to her fellow-creatures as if saying—'Behold, I am sinking, bare of help: ye must help me! I am your sister, bone of your bone; one God made us: ye must help me!' They answer—'No; impossible: thou art no sister of ours.' But she proves her sisterhood; *her* typhus fever kills *them;* they actually were her brothers, though denying it!"

And so are these multitudes flocking to our shores our brethren, our sisters. Ignorant, degraded, as many of them are, they are yet sharers of our nature, and if we refuse them our aid, they will prove it, even as did the poor Irish widow, for their ignorance and vice shall infect us; or if our matured powers resist the influence of the moral malaria they create, our children shall fall victims to it.

But, perhaps some will say, "We see the truth as you do; the course you suggest is noble, the goal to which it leads, 'a consummation devoutly to be wished;' but we have wandered too far from that course to return to it—between our present position and that to which you would point us, lies a great gulf, a gulf which we dare not even attempt to pass." To such persons we reply, if you do indeed acknowledge that your present position is wrong—that, having once occupied it, you can never hope to attain to that beauty and nobleness which your soul perceives and admires, and for which, as this very admiration proves, you were created—strive to win for your children at least, that better part. You shudder at those Pagans who cast their children into the cold waters of the Ganges, or the fiery embrace of Moloch, yet, by all the influences of your present life, you are preparing for yours, not a death-pang short—though sharp, followed by a certain entrance into the Paradise of your faith —but an eternity of icy selfishness or burning passion.

Look at the young immortal as it lies so fresh and fair within your arms, the purity of heaven on its brow, and nothing of earth within its heart but the love with which it leaps to the sound of the mother-voice and the tender smile of the mother-eyes; in that little being, scarce yet conscious of existence, are enfolded powers to bless or to curse, extended as the universe, enduring as eternity. The hand which now clings so feebly, yet so tenaciously, to your own, may uphold or overthrow an empire—the voice whose weak cry scarce wins the attention of any but a mother's ear, may one day stir a nation's heart, and give the first impulse to actions which will hasten or retard for ages the world's millennial glories. And will you, nay, *dare* you strive to compress these powers to the dimensions of a drawing-room, and to present its paltry triumphs as the highest reward of their exercise?

The daughter whose bounding step and joyous prattle make the music of your home—shall she walk through the world's dark and troubled ways, an angel of charity, blessing and blessed, warming into life by her cordial sympathies, all those pure, unselfish affections, by which we know ourselves allied to heaven, but which fade, and too often die in the atmosphere of earth—shall "her path be as that of the just, shining more and more unto the perfect day," and shall she pass at length gently, serenely, with peace in her soul, from her earthly home to that fairer home above of which she has made it no unworthy type?—or, shall she be the belle of one, two, or it may be, three seasons, nurturing in herself and others the baleful passions of envy and hate, of impurity and pride? Shall her life, with all its capabilities of good and ill, of joy and sorrow, be devoted to frivolities which she would herself blush to acknowledge as her aim; and shall death find her in the midst of such pursuits, and bear her, vainly struggling—whither? Do you shrink from such a picture? Do you ask, how may we secure for our children the first and nobler destiny? It is a question of deep and solemn import, for whose full answer we must direct you to the Book of Life; but some things are so obviously necessary to your feeblest efforts to attain such a result, that we will not hesitate to state them. And first, you must cease to regard your children as instruments for the gratification of your own vanity. Torture not the childish form, instil not the poison of envy and vanity into the childish heart, that your ear may be soothed by the soft flatteries of some fashionable circle. Is your child clothed with a plain exterior—neither depress her by your regret, nor seek to win for her, by the splendor of her dress, an admiration which her person would fail to excite. Rather, teach her that there is a loveliness more to be desired than any external beauty, and that the ornament of a meek and quiet spirit is of more price than rubies. Is she beautiful—teach her that this, too, like every other gift of Heaven, is valuable only for the good it may enable us to do, only as a means of influence over other hearts.

In physical education be more careful of health than of fashion; we do not say of beauty, for between the laws of health and of beauty there is no want of harmony, while fashion often contradicts both. It requires little reflection to perceive what must be the influence on a child's mind of having the free movements of nature impeded, and present discomfort and the apprehension of future disease inflicted on her, that her form may be forced into the mould prescribed by the caprice of *ton*.

As the first dawn of childhood brightens into day—as the faculties expand and the observation is quickened—you can no longer hope to form your child to a nobler life, while you continue yourself to tread the beaten round of frivolous amusements and selfish pleasures. How can you preface a day devoted to such objects, by the lesson that we were created to be co-workers with God in the elevation of our own natures and those of our brethren; that the day has been lost to us in which we have accomplished no useful work, subtracted nothing from the evil, or added nothing to the good, in our world? Should you even summon courage to utter such sentiments, contradicted as they would be by every hour of your lives, could you expect them to make any impression on the minds to which they would be addressed? Surely not.

If it be indeed impossible to make your life a fit model, and your home a fit school for the inculcation of the principles you approve, you must be content to see the lives of your children shadowed by the clouds which have settled so darkly over your own; to see their earnest purposes and nobler aspirations exchanged for the false and the frivolous conventionalisms, of which you have learned, by your own sad experience, that their charm soon ceases, and their despotism never ends; or you must sacrifice their society, and seek for them a model and a home elsewhere. Schools there are—and we rejoice to believe that they are becoming more numerous—in which the principles of a true Christian civilization are inculcated, in which the young are taught that no extrinsic advantages of wealth or station will atone for the want of those personal qualities that command respect—schools in which the rich and the poor meet together, and that pupil is most prized who promises, by the highest intellectual power and the purest moral principle, to make the most useful member of society. It is by the pupils of such schools, that the American life—a life of usefulness, of true refinement, and of wise philanthropy—must be instituted and sustained. In the support of such schools, therefore, we find the most en couraging promise for the future destiny of our country and of the world.

We are not advocating the principles of a savage democracy; we would not, if we could, force into uncongenial association intelligence and ignorance, rudeness and refinement. We have spoken of the union of the laboring hand with the thoughtful mind and the cultivated manner, but we have nowhere insinuated the desire to see vulgarity and refinement brought into unnatural connection. We would set in motion influences by which vulgarity, whether clothed in the garb of prince or peasant, whether seated in high places or plodding through lanes and fields, should be banished from our land. We desire that the arrangements of our social life may be such that each, in his own sphere, may have room to develop himself freely, and with such aids as will give to that development a right direction. Esteeming the glorious ray kindled by the breath of the Almighty beyond the feeble glimmer of a diamond, we would have our social life adapted to cherish and to exhibit the spirit which dwells in man, rather than the clothing which envelops him. We would have our conventional arrangements so modified as no longer to press out of sight all that is noblest among us; no longer to set up a golden calf for worship in the very presence of the most sublime manifestations of the Divine Spirit; no longer, by making idleness and display the terms of social distinction, at once to stimulate the passion for wealth and check the honest and lawful efforts for its acquisition, giving birth to wild speculations and fraudulent practices, to misery, and madness, and crime.

It has been said that in our land, the child of the rich man is often father to the poor man. This more than usual instability of fortune is probably the result of that ambition for display to which we have already so often alluded. We note it now, however, not to investigate its cause, but to use it as an incentive to all, in the midst of riches, to cultivate in themselves and in their children, consideration for those less fortunate. Let them remember that their children, or their children's children, may reap the benefit of the general inculcation of such a sentiment.

A motive nobler but less influential, we fear, might be found in that patriotism which has become in modern times a word of light value. We are told sometimes that this is an emotion incompatible with that universal philanthropy inculcated by the gospel of Christ. We fear, however, that we have exchanged the old Roman devotion to our own land, not for a wider but for a narrower sentiment—for one which begins, continues, and ends, in self. The objects which we have commended should be alike dear to us as Americans and as Christian philanthropists, since they would prepare our country, by the influence of a thorough public instruction and the more enduring influence of its homes, to become the source of blessing to the world.

The dignity of labor, the superiority of a civilization which shall look to the moral and intellectual cultivation of all, over that which presents evidence of the refinements in luxury and art enjoyed by a few; these are the ideas we have striven to enforce. The conception still stands before us—noble, beautiful, as when first it lured us to undertake its presentation. The task has been fulfilled, imperfectly we are conscious, yet with an honest, earnest effort. The world's rushing tide may drown our feeble voice for a time, but if we have spoken true words, as we believe, they will not be lost; some faint echo of their tone may perchance fall on the ear and stir the heart of one who will give them worthier utterance. So BE IT.

THE END.

HISTORICAL AND BIOGRAPHICAL WORKS.

ARNOLD, (Dr.) Early History of Rome. 2 vols. 8vo. - - - $5 00

ARNOLD, (Dr.) History of the Later Roman Commonwealth. 8vo. - - - - - - - 2 50

ARNOLD, (Dr.) Lectures on Modern History, edited by Professor Reed. 12mo. - - - - 1 25

ARNOLD, (Dr.) Life and Correspondence, by the Rev. A. P. Stanley. 2d ed. 8vo. - - 2 00

BURNETT'S History of the North-western Territory. 8vo. - - 2 50

CARLYLE'S Life of Schiller. A new edition. 12mo. - - - - 75

COIT'S History of Puritanism. 12mo. - - - - - - - 1 00

EVELYN'S Life of Mrs. Godolphin, edited by Bishop of Oxford. 12mo - - - - - - 50

FROST, (Professor) History of the United States Navy. Plates. 12mo. 1 00

FROST, (Professor) History of the United States Army. Plates. 12mo. - - - - - - - 1 00

FROST, (Professor) History of the Indians of North America. Plates. 12mo. - - - - - - 1 00

FROST, (Professor) History of the Colonies of America. 12mo. Illustrated - - - - - - 1 00

FROST, (Professor) Life of Gen. Zachary Taylor. 12mo. Illustrated. - - - - - - - 1 25

GUIZOT'S History of Civilization in Europe, edited by Professor Henry. 12mo - - - - 1 00

GUIZOT'S Complete History of Civilization, translated by Hazlett. 4 vols. - - - - - 3 50

GUIZOT'S History of the English Revolution, 1640. 12mo. - - 1 25

GAYARRE'S Romance of the History of Louisiana. 12mo. - - 1 00

HULL, (General) Military and Civil Life. 8vo. - - - - - 2 00

KING, (Colonel) History of the Argentine Republic. 12mo. - 75

KOHLRAUSCH'S Complete History of Germany. 8vo. - - - 1 50

MAHON'S (Lord) History of England, edited by Professor Reed. 2 vols., 8vo. - - - - - 5 00

MICHELET'S History of France from the Earliest Period. 2 vols. 5 50

MICHELET'S History of the Roman Republic. 12mo. - - 90

MICHELET'S History of the People. 12mo. - - - 63

MICHELET'S Life of Martin Luther. 12mo. - - - - $0 7

NAPOLEON, Life of, from the French of Laurent De L'Ardeche. 2 vols. 8vo. 500 cuts - - 4 00

O'CALLAGHAN'S Early History of New York. 2 vols. 8vo. - 5 00

ROWAN'S History of the French Revolution. 18mo. 2 vols. in 1 63

SEWELL'S Child's History of Rome. 18mo. - - - - - 50

SOUTHEY'S Life of Oliver Cromwell. 18mo. - - - - - 38

SPRAGUE'S History of the Florida War. Map and Plates. 8vo. 2 50

STEVEN'S History of Georgia. vol. 1 - - - - - - - 2 50

TAYLOR'S Natural History of Society in the Barbarous and Civilized State. 2 vols. 12mo. - 2 25

TAYLOR'S Manual of Ancient and Modern History. Edited by Professor Henry. 8vo. - - 2 50

TAYLOR'S Ancient History—Separate - - - - - - - 1 25

TAYLOR'S Modern History—Separate - - - - - - 1 50

Used as a Text-book in several Colleges.

TWISS. History of the Oregon Territory. 12mo. - - - - 75

LAW BOOKS.

ANTHON'S Law Student ; or, Guides to the Study of the Law in its Principles.

HOLCOMBE'S Digest of the Decisions of the Supreme Court of the U. S., from its Commencement to the present time. Large 8vo., law sheep - - - 6 00

HOLCOMBE'S Supreme Court Leading Cases on Commercial Law. 8vo., law sheep - - 4 00

HOLCOMBE'S Law of Debtor and Creditor in the United States and Canada. 8vo. - - - - 3 50

SMITH'S Compendium of Mercantile Law. With Large American Additions, by Holcombe and Gholson. 8vo., law sheep - 4 00

These volumes are highly commended by Justices Taney and Woodbury, Daniel Webster, Rufus Choate, and Chancellor Kent, &c.

WARREN'S Popular and Practical Introduction to Law Studies. With American additions, by Thomas W. Clerke. 8vo., law sheep - - - - - - - 2 50

MISCELLANEOUS.

ACTON, or the Circle of Life. $1 25
AGNELL'S Book of Chess. A Complete Guide to the Game. Steel Illustrations. 12mo. - 1 50
APPLETONS' Library Manual; a valuable book of reference for the book buyer and seller. 500 pp., 8vo., paper cover, $1; half roan 1 25
APPLETONS' New and Complete United States Traveller's Guide, including the Canadas, &c. Nearly 50 Maps. 16mo.
APPLETONS' Southern & Western Guide, with Maps of the Routes and Plans of the Principal Cities. 16mo. 1 00
APPLETONS' Northern and Eastern Traveller's Guide, with 30 Maps of Routes, Plans of Cities, &c. 16mo. - - - - - 1 25
ARNOLD'S Miscellaneous Works 2 00
BALLET GIRL, The Natural History of. By Albert Smith. With Illustrations. 18mo. - - 25
BLANCHARD'S Heads and Tales of Travellers. 18mo. - - 25
CHAPMAN'S Instructions on the Use of the American Rifle - 1 25
DELEUZE'S Treatise on Animal Magnetism - - - - 1 00
ELLIS'S Mothers, Daughters, and Women of England. Each - 50
FROST (Professor). Book of Good Examples. 12mo. Illustrated - 1 00
FROST. Book of Anecdotes. 12mo. Illustrated - - - - 1 00
FROST. Book of Illustrious Mechanics. 12mo. Illustrated - 1 00
GENT, (The Natural History of). By Albert Smith. Illustrated - 25
GRANT'S Memoirs of an American Lady. 12mo - - - 75
GUIZOT'S Democracy in France - 25
HOBSON. My Uncle Hobson & I. 50
KIP'S Christmas Holidays in Rome. 12mo. - - - 1 00
LAMB'S Final Memorials. Edited by Talfourd. 12mo. - - 75
LANMAN'S Summer in the Wilderness. 12mo. - - - 63
LEGER'S History of Animal Magnetism. 12mo. - - - 1 25
POWELL'S Living Authors of England. 12mo. - - - 1 00
REPUBLIC of the United States. Its Duties, &c. 12mo. - - 75
ROGET'S Economic Chess Board Companion, in Case - $ 50
SAWYER'S Plea for Amusement 50
SELECT Italian Comedies. 12mo. 1 00
SOMETHING FOR EVERY BODY. By Robert Carlton. 12mo. 75
SOUTHGATE (Bishop). Visit to Syrian Church - - - 1 00
TUCKERMAN'S American Artist Life - - - - - - - 75
WANDERINGS in the Western World; or, the European in America - - - - - 75
WAYLAND'S Real Life in England - - - - - - - 38
WHIPPLE'S Essays and Reviews. 2 vols. 12mo. - - - 2 25
WARNER'S Rudimental Lessons in Music. 18mo. - - - 50
———— Primary Note Reader 25
WOMAN'S WORTH; or Hints to Raise the Female Character. By a Lady. 18mo. - - - 38

SCIENCE AND USEFUL ARTS.

ANSTED'S Gold Seeker's Manual. 12mo. - - - - - 25
ARNOT'S Gothic Architecture, applied to Modern Residences. Parts, each - - - - 25
BOURNE'S Catechism of the Steam Engine. 18mo. - 75
BOUISSANGAULT'S Rural Economy - - - - - 1 50
BYRNE'S New Method of Calculating Logarithms. 16mo. - 1 00
———— Dictionary of Machine, Mechanic Engine Work. Publishing. In numbers, each - - 25
COOLEY'S Cyclopædia of 6000 Practical Receipts, in all branches of Arts, Manufactures, and Trades - - - - 2 25
FALKNER'S Farmer's Manual. 50
FARMER'S TREASURE. (The) A Manual of Agriculture - 75
FRESENIUS' Qualitative Chemical Analysis - - - - 1 00
HODGE on the Steam Engine. 48 plates - - - - - 10 00
HALLECK'S Elements of Military Art and Science. Illus. 1 50
LEFEVRE'S Beauties of Modern Architecture. 48 Plates - 6 00
MARSHALL'S Farmer's Hand Book - - - - - 1 00
MILES on the Horse's Foot - 25
PARNELL'S Chemistry applied to the Arts - - - - 1 00
STEWART'S Stable Economy - 1 00
THOMSON on the Food of Animals and Man - - - - 50
URE'S Dictionary of Arts and Sciences, with Supplement. New edition. 1 vol. - - - 5 00
WILSON on Healthy Skin. Illus. 1 00

ILLUSTRATED STANDARD POETS.

HALLECK'S COMPLETE POETICAL WORKS. Beautifully illustrated with fine Steel Engravings and a Portrait. 1 vol. 8vo., finest paper, cloth extra, gilt edges, $3; morocco extra, $5; morocco antique, $6.

BYRON'S COMPLETE POETICAL WORKS. Illustrated with elegant Steel Engravings and Portrait. 1 vol. 8vo., fine paper, cloth, $4; cloth, gilt leaves, $4 50; morocco extra, $6 50.

Cheaper edition, with Portrait and Vignette, $2 50.

MOORE'S COMPLETE POETICAL WORKS. Illustrated with very fine Steel Engravings and Portrait. 1 vol. 8vo., fine paper, cloth, $4; cloth, gilt edges, $5; morocco extra, $7.

Cheaper edition, with Portrait and Vignette, $2 50.

SOUTHEY'S COMPLETE POETICAL WORKS. Illustrated with several beautiful Steel Engravings. 1 vol. 8vo., fine paper, cloth, $3 50; cloth, gilt edges, $4 50; morocco extra, $6 50.

SACRED POETS (The) of England and America, for Three Centuries. Edited by Rufus W. Griswold. Illustrated with Steel Engravings. 1 vol. 8vo., cloth $2 50; gilt edges, $3; morocco, $3 50; morocco extra, $4.

POEMS BY AMELIA. New and enlarged edition, beautifully illustrated with original designs, by Weir, and Portrait of the Author. 1 vol. 8vo., cloth extra, gilt edges, $3; morocco extra, $4; morocco antique, $5: 12mo., without Plates, $1 25; gilt edges, $1 50.

No expense has been spared in the mechanical execution of the above popular standard authors.

CABINET EDITIONS.

CAMPBELL'S COMPLETE POETICAL WORKS. Illustrated with Steel Engravings and a Portrait. 16mo., cloth, $1 50; gilt edges, $2 25; morocco extra, $3.

BUTLER'S HUDIBRAS, with Notes by Nash. Illustrated with Portraits. 16mo., cloth, $1 50; gilt edges, $2 25; morocco extra, $3.

DANTE'S POEMS. Translated by Cary. Illustrated with a fine Portrait and 12 Engravings. 16mo., cloth, $1 50; gilt edges, $2 25; morocco extra, $3.

TASSO'S JERUSALEM DELIVERED. Translated by Wiffen. Illustrated with a Portrait and Steel Engravings. 1 vol. 16mo. Uniform with "Dante." Cloth, $1 50; gilt edges, $2 25; morocco, $3.

BYRON'S CHILDE HAROLD'S PILGRIMAGE. 16mo. Illustrated, cloth, $1 25; gilt edges, $2; morocco extra, $2 50.

BURNS' COMPLETE POETICAL WORKS, with Life, Glossary, &c. 16mo., cloth, illustrated, $1 25; gilt edges, $2; morocco extra, $2 50.

COWPER'S COMPLETE POETICAL WORKS, with Life, &c. Morocco extra, 2 vols. in 1, $3; cloth, $1 50; gilt edges, $2 50.

MILTON'S COMPLETE POETICAL WORKS, with Life, &c. 16mo., cloth, illustrated, $1 25; gilt edges, $2; morocco extra, $2 50.

SCOTT'S POETICAL WORKS, with Life, &c. Cloth, 16mo., illustrated, $1 25; gilt edges, $2; morocco extra, $2 50.

HEMANS' COMPLETE POETICAL WORKS. Edited by her Sister. 2 vols., 16mo., with 10 Steel Plates, cloth, $2 50; gilt edges, $4; Turkey morocco, $5.

POPE'S POETICAL WORKS. Illustrated with 24 Steel Engravings. 16mo., cloth, $1 50; gilt edges, $2 25; morocco, $3.

RELIGIOUS WORKS.

ARNOLD'S Rugby School Sermons - . . - - -$ 50
ANTHON'S Catechism on the Homilies - - - - - - 06
ANTHON'S Easy Catechism for Young Children - - - 06
A KEMPIS. Of the Imitation of Christ - - - - - - 75
BURNET'S History of the Reformation. Edited by Dr. Nares. 23 Portraits. 4 vols. - - 6 00
Do. Cheap edition. 3 vols. - 2 50
BURNET on the Thirty-nine Articles. Best edition - - 2 00
BEAVEN'S Help to Catechising. Edited by Dr. Anthon - - 06
BRADLEY'S Parochial and Practical Sermons. 4 vols. in 1 - 2 00
CRUDEN'S Concordance to the New Testament - - - - 50
COTTER. The Romish Mass and Rubrics. Translated - - 38
CHRISTMAS Bells and other Poems - - - - - - - 50
COIT, Dr. Puritanism Reviewed 1 00
EVANS' Rectory of Valehead - 50
FABER on the Doctrine of Election . - - - - - 1 50
FOUR GOSPELS, arranged as a Practical Family Commentary for Every Day in the Year. 8vo. Illustrated - - - - 2 00
FOSTERS' Essay on Christian Morals - - - - - - 50
GRESLEY'S Portrait of an English Churchman - - - - 50
GRESLEY'S TREATISE on Preaching - - - - - 1 25
HOOK. The Cross of Christ; Meditations on our Saviour - 50
HOOKER'S Complete Works. Edited by Keble. 2 vols. - - 4 50
IVES, Bishop. Sermons. 16mo. 50
JARVIS. Reply to Milner's End of Controversy. 12mo. - 75
KEBLE'S Christian Year, handsomely printed - - - 75
KINGSLEY'S Sacred Choir - 75
LAYMAN'S Lesson to a Lord Bishop on Sacerdotal Powers. 12mo. 25
LYRA Apostolica. 18mo. - - 50
MARSHALL'S Notes on Episcopacy. Edited by Wainwright - 1 00
MANNING on the Unity of the Church. 16mo. - - - - 75
MAGEE on Atonement and Sacrifice. 2 vols. 8vo. - - - 5 00
MORELL'S Philosophy of Religion. 12mo. - - - - $1 25
MOCHLER'S Symbolics. 8vo. - 2 25
NEWMAN'S Sermons on Sjubects of the Day - - - - 1 00
NEWMAN'S Essay on Christian Doctrine. 8vo. Paper cover, 25 cts.; cloth - - - - - - 50
OGILBY'S Lectures on the Church. 16mo. - - - - - - 50
OGILBY on Lay Baptism. 12mo. 50
PAGET'S Tales of the Village. 3 vols. 16mo. - - - - 1 25
PALMER on the Church. Edited by Bishop Whittingham. 2 vols. 5 00
PEARSON on the Creed. Edited by Dobson. 8vo. - - - 2 00
PULPIT Cyclopædia and Minister's Companion. 8vo., 600 pp., $2 50; sheep - - - - 2 75
PSALTER, (The) or Psalms of David, pointed for chanting. Edited by Dr. Muhlenberg. 12mo., 38c.; sheep - - - - 50
SOUTHARD, "The Mystery of Godliness." 8vo. - - - 75
SKETCHES and Skeletons of 500 Sermons. By the Author of "The Pulpit Cyclopædia." 8vo. - 2 50
SPENCER'S Christian Instructed 1 00
SHERLOCK'S Practical Christian 71
SPINCKE'S Manual of Private Devotion - - - - - - 71
SUTTON'S Disce Vivere, Learn to Live. 16mo. - - - - 75
SWARTZ. Letters to my Godchild. 32mo. - - - - - 38
TRENCH'S Notes on the Miracles 1 75
TAYLOR'S Golden Grove - 50
TAYLOR'S Holy Living and Dying - - - - - - - - 1 00
TAYLOR'S Episcopacy Asserted and Maintained - - - 75
WILBERFORCE'S Manual for Communicants - - - - - 38
WILSON'S Lectures on Colossians. 12mo. - - - - 75
WILSON'S Sacra Privata. 16mo. 75
WHISTON'S Constitution of the Holy Apostles, including the Canons. Translated by Doctor Chase 8vo. - - - - 2 50
WYATT'S Christian Altar - 38

BOOK OF COMMON PRAYER. New Standard Edition. The Book of Common Prayer and Administration of the Sacraments and other Rites and Ceremonies of the Church, according to the use of the Protestant Episcopal Church in the United States of America, together with the Psalter or Psalms of David Illustrated with Steel Engravings by Overbeck, and a finely illuminated title-page, in various elegant bindings. Five different sizes.

COLLEGE AND SCHOOL TEXT-BOOKS.

I. Greek and Latin.

ARNOLD'S First and Second Latin Book and Practical Grammar. 12mo. - - - $ 75

ARNOLD'S Latin Prose Composition. 12mo. - - - - 1 00

ARNOLD'S Cornelius Nepos. With Notes. 12mo. - - 1 00

ARNOLD'S First Greek Book - 62

ARNOLD'S Greek Prose Composition. 12mo. - - - 75

ARNOLD'S Greek Reading Book. Edited by Spencer. 12mo. - 1 50

BEZA'S Latin Testament. 12mo. 63

BOISE'S Exercises in Greek Prose Composition. 12mo. - - 75

CÆSAR'S Commentaries. Notes by Spencer. 12mo. - - 1 00

CICERO'S Select Orations. Notes by Johnson. 12mo.

CICERO De Senectute and De Amicitia. Notes by Johnson. 12mo. (*In Press.*)

CICERO De Officiis. Notes by Thatcher 12mo.

HORACE, with Notes by Lincoln. 12mo. (*In Press.*)

LIVY, with Notes by Lincoln. 12mo. - - - - - 1 00

SALLUST, with Notes by Butler. 12mo. (*In Press.*)

TACITUS'S Histories. Notes by Tyler. 12mo. - - - 1 25

——— Germania and Agricola. Notes by Tyler. 12mo. - 62

II. Hebrew.

GESENIUS'S Hebrew Grammar. Edited by Rödiger. Translated from the best German edition, by Conant. 8vo. - - - 2 00

III. English.

ARNOLD'S Lectures on Modern History. 12mo. - - - 1 25

BOJESON and Arnold's Manual of Greek and Roman Antiquities. 12mo. - - - - - - 1 00

CROSBY'S First Lessons in Geometry. 16mo. - - - 38

CHARE'S Treatise on Algebra. 12mo - - - - - - 1 00

EVERETT'S System of English Versification. 12mo. - $ 75

GRAHAM'S English Synonymes. Edited by Professor Reed, of Pa. University. 12mo. - 1

GUIZOT'S History of Civilization. Notes by Professor Henry, of N. Y. University. 12mo. - - 1 00

HOWS' Shaksper. Reader. 12mo 1 25

JAGER'S Class Book of Zoology. 18mo. - - - - - - 42

KEIGHTLEY'S Mythology of Greece and Rome. 18mo. - 42

MAGNALL'S Histor. Questions. With American additions. 12mo. 1 00

MARKHAM'S School History of England. Edited by Eliza Robins, author of "Popular Lessons." 12mo. - - - - - 75

MANDEVILLE'S Series of School Readers:

——— Part I. - - 10

——— Part II. - - 16

——— Part III. - - 25

——— Part IV. - 38

——— Course of Reading for Common Schools and Lower Academies. 12mo. - 75

——— Elements of Reading and Oratory. 8vo. - 1 00

PUTZ and ARNOLD'S Manual of Ancient Geography and History. 12mo. - - - - - 1 00

REID'S Dictionary of the English Language, with Derivations, &c. 12mo. - - - - - - 1 00

SEWELL'S First History of Rome. 16mo. - - - - - - 50

TAYLOR'S Manual of Modern and Ancient History. Edited by Professor Henry. 8vo., cloth or sheep - - - - - 2 50

TAYLOR'S Ancient History. Separate - - - - - - 1 25

TAYLOR'S Modern ditto - - 1 50

WRIGHT'S Primary Lessons; or Child's First Book - - - 13

In Press.

GREEN'S (Profesor) Manual of the Geography and History of the Middle Ages. 12mo.

BURNHAM'S New Mental and Written Arithmetic.

TEXT BOOKS

FOR LEARNING THE FRENCH, GERMAN, ITALIAN, AND SPANISH LANGUAGES.

I. FRENCH.

COLLOT'S Dramatic French Reader. 12mo. $1.

DE FIVA'S Elementary French Reader. 12mo. 50 cts.

DE FIVA'S Classic French Reader for Advanced Students. 12mo. $1.

OLLENDORFF'S Elementary French Grammar. By Greene. 16mo. 38 cts. with Key, 50 cts.

OLLENDORFF'S New Method of Learning French. Edited by J. L. Jewett. 12mo. $1.

KEY to ditto. 75 cts.

ROWAN'S Modern French Reader. 12mo. 75 cts.

SURRENNE'S French Pronouncing Dictionary. 12mo. $1 50.

VALUE'S New and Easy System of Learning French. 12mo. (*In Press.*)

NEW and COMPLETE FRENCH and ENGLISH DICTIONARY. 1 vol. 8vo To match Adler's German Lexicon. (*In Press.*)

II. GERMAN.

ADLER'S Progressive German Reader. 12mo. $1.

GERMAN and English, and English and German Dictionary, compiled from the best authorities. 1 vol. large 8vo. $5.

EICHORN'S New Practical German Grammar. 12mo. $1.

OLLENDORFF'S New Method of Learning German. Edited by G. J. Adler 12mo. $1 50.

III. ITALIAN.

FORESTI'S Italian Reader. 12mo. $1.

OLLENDORFF'S New Method of Learning Italian. Edited by F. Foresti. 12mo. $1 50.

KEY to ditto 75 cts.

IV. SPANISH.

OLLENDORFF'S New Method of Learning Spanish. By M. Velasquez and T. Simonne. 12mo. $1 50.

KEY to ditto, 75 cts.

PALENZUELA'S new Grammar on the Ollendorff System, for Spaniards to Learn English. (*In Press.*)

VELASQUEZ'S New Spanish Reader. With Lexicon. 12mo. $1 25.

VELASQUEZ'S New Spanish Phrase Book; or Conversations in English and Spanish. 18mo. 38 cts.

VELASQUEZ'S and SEOANE'S New Spanish and English, and English and Spanish Dictionary. Large 8vo. To match "Adler's German Lexicon." (*In Press.*)

NOVELS AND TALES.

CORBOULD'S History and Adventures of Margaret Catchpole. 8vo. 2 Plates. 25 cts.
DON QUIXOTTE de la Mancha. Translated from the Spanish. Illustrated with 18 Steel Engravings. 16mo, cloth. $1 50.
DUMAS' Marguerite de Valois. A Novel. 8vo. 25 cts.
ELLEN MIDDLETON. A Tale. By Lady Fullerton. 12mo. 75 cts.
FRIENDS AND FORTUNE. A Moral Tale. By Miss Dewey. 12mo. 75 cts.
GOLDSMITH'S Vicar of Wakefield. Illustrated. 12mo. 75 cts.
GRACE LESLIE. A Tale. 12mo. 75 cts.
GRANTLEY MANOR. A Tale. By Lady Fullerton. 12mo. Paper, 50 cts. cloth, 75 cts.
LADY ALICE; or, The New Una. 8vo. Paper, 38 cts.
LAMARTINE'S Les Confidences et Raphael. 8vo. $1.
LAMARTINE'S CONFIDENTIAL DISCLOSURES. 12mo. 50 cts.
LOVER'S (Samuel) Handy Andy. 8vo. Paper, 50 cts.
———— £ s. d. Treasure Trove. 8vo. Paper, 25 cts.
MACKINTOSH (M. J.) Two Lives; or, To Seem and To Be. 12mo. Paper 50 cts.; cloth, 75 cts.
———— Aunt Kitty's Tales. 12mo. Paper, 50 cts.; cloth, 75 cts.
———— Charms and Counter Charms. Paper, 75 cts.; cloth, $1.
MAXWELL'S Way-side and Border Sketches. 8vo. 25 cts.
———— Fortunes of Hector O'Halloran. 8vo. 50 cts.
MANZONI. The Betrothed Lovers. 2 vols. 12mo. $1 50.
MAIDEN AUNT (The). By S. M. 12mo. 75 cts.
SEWELL (Miss). Amy Herbert. A Tale. 12mo. Paper, 50 cts.; cloth, 75 cts.
———— Gertrude. A Tale. 12mo. Paper, 50 cts.; cloth, 75 cts.
———— Laneton Parsonage. 3 vols. 12mo. Paper, $1 50; cloth, $2 25.
———— Margaret Percival. 2 vols. Paper, $1; cloth, $1 50.
———— Walter Lorimer, and other Tales. 12mo. 75 cts.
TAYLOR, (General) Anecdote Book, Letters, &c. 8vo. 25 cts.
ZSCHOKKE. Incidents of Social Life. 12mo. $1.

MINIATURE CLASSICAL LIBRARY.

Published in elegant form, with Frontispiece.

POETICAL LACON; or Aphorisms from the Poets. 38 cts.
BOND'S Golden Maxims. 31 cts.
CLARKE'S Scripture Promises. Complete. 38 cts.
ELIZABETH; or the Exiles of Siberia. 31 cts.
GOLDSMITH'S Vicar of Wakefield. 38 cts.
———— Essays. 38 cts.
GEMS from American Poets. 38 cts.
HANNAH MORE'S Private Devotions. 31 cts.
———— Practical Piety. 2 vols. 75 cts.
HEMANS' Domestic Affections. 31 cts
HOFFMAN'S Lays of the Hudson, &c. 38 cts.
JOHNSON'S History of Rasselas. 38 cts.
MANUAL of Matrimony. 31 cts.
MOORE'S Lallah Rookh. 38 cts.
———— Melodies. Complete. 38 cts.
PAUL and Virginia. 31 cts.
POLLOK'S Course of Time. 38 cts.
PURE Gold from the Rivers of Wisdom. 38 cts.
THOMSON'S Seasons. 38 cts.
TOKEN of the Heart.—Do. of Affection.—Do. of Remembrance.—Do of Friendship.—Do. of Love; each, 31 cts.
USEFUL Letter Writer. 38 cts.
WILSON'S Sacra Privata. 31 cts.
Young's Night Thoughts. 38 cts.

PROF. MANDEVILLE'S READING BOOKS.

I. PRIMARY, OR FIRST READER. Price 10 cents.

II. SECOND READER. Price 16 cents.

These two Readers are formed substantially on the same plan; and the second is a continuation of the first. The design of both is, to combine a knowledge of the meaning and pronunciation of words, with a knowledge of their grammatical functions. The parts of speech are introduced successively, beginning with the articles, these are followed by the demonstrative pronouns; and these again by others, class after class, until all that are requisite to form a sentence have been separately considered; when the common reading lessons begin.

The Second Reader reviews the ground passed over in the Primary, but adds largely to the amount of information. The child is here also taught to read writing as well as printed matter; and in the reading lessons, attention is constantly directed to the different ways in which sentences are formed and connected, and of the peculiar manner in which each of them is delivered. All who have examined these books, have pronounced them a decided and important advance on every other of the same class in use.

III. THIRD READER. Price 25 cents.

IV. FOURTH READER. Price 38 cents.

In the first two Readers, the main object is to make the pupil acquainted with the meaning and functions of words, and to impart facility in pronouncing them in sentential connection: the leading design of these, is to form a natural, flexible, and varied delivery. Accordingly, the Third Reader opens with a series of exercises on articulation and modulation, containing numerous examples for practice on the elementary sounds (including errors to be corrected) and on the different movements of the voice, produced by sentential structure, by emphasis, and by the passions. The habits formed by these exercises, which should be thoroughly, as they can be easily mastered, under intelligent instruction, find scope for improvement and confirmation in the reading lessons which follow, in the same book and that which succeeds.

These lessons have been selected with special reference to the following peculiarities: 1st. Colloquial character; 2d, Variety of sentential structure; 3d, Variety of subject matter; 4th Adaptation to the progressive development of the pupil's mind; and, as far as possible, 5th, Tendency to excite moral and religious emotions. Great pains have been taken to make the books in these respects, which are, in fact, characteristic of the whole series, superior to any others in use; with what success, a brief comparison will readily show.

V. THE FIFTH READER; OR, COURSE OF READING. Price 75 cents.

VI. THE ELEMENTS OF READING AND ORATORY. Price $1.

These books are designed to cultivate the literary taste, as well as the understanding and vocal powers of the pupil.

THE COURSE OF READING comprises three parts; the *first part* containing a more elaborate description of elementary sounds and the parts of speech grammatically considered than was deemed necessary in the preceding works; here indispensable: *part second*, a complete classification and description of every sentence to be found in the English, or any other language; examples of which in every degree of expansion, from a few words to the half of an octavo page in length, are adduced, and arranged to be read; and as each species has its peculiar delivery as well as structure, both are learned at the same time; *part third*, paragraphs; or sentences in their connection unfolding general thoughts, as in the common reading books. It may be observed that the selections of sentences in part second, and of paragraphs in part third, comprise some of the finest gems in the language: distinguished alike for beauty of thought and facility of diction. If not found in a school book, they might be appropriately called "elegant extracts"

The ELEMENTS OF READING AND ORATORY closes the series with an exhibition of the whole theory and art of Elocution exclusive of gesture. It contains, besides the classification of sentences already referred to, but here presented with fuller statement and illustration, the laws of punctuation and delivery deduced from it: the whole followed by carefully selected pieces for sentential analysis and vocal practice.

THE RESULT.—The student who acquaints himself thoroughly with the contents of this book, will, as numerous experiments have proved; 1st, Acquire complete knowledge of the structure of the language; 2d, Be able to designate any sentence of any book by name at a glance; 3d, Be able to declare with equal rapidity its proper punctuation; 4th, Be able to delare, and with sufficient practice to give its proper delivery. Such are a few of the general characteristics of the series of school books which the publishers now offer to the friends and patrons of a sound common school and academic education. For more particular information, reference is respectfully made to the "Hints," which may be found at the beginning of each volume.

N. B. The punctuation in all these books conforms, in the main, to the sense and proper delivery of every sentence, and is a guide to both. When a departure from the proper punctuation occurs, the proper delivery is indicated. As reading books are usually punctuated, it is a matter of surprise that children should learn to read at all.

*** The above series of Reading Books are already very extensively introduced and commended by the most experienced Teachers in the country. "Prof. Mandeville's system is eminently original, scientific and practical, and destined wherever it is introduced to supersede at once all others."

DR. ARNOLD'S WORKS.

I.

THE HISTORY OF ROME,

From the Earliest Period. Reprinted entire from the last English edition, Two vols., 8vo. $5 00.

II.

HISTORY OF THE LATER ROMAN COMMONWEALTH.

Two vols. of the English edition reprinted entire in 1 vol., 8vo. $2 50.

"The History of Rome will remain, to the latest age of the world, the most attractive, the most useful, and the most elevating subject of human contemplation. It must ever form the basis of a liberal and enlightened education, and present the most important subject to the contemplation of the statesman. It is remarkable, that until the appearance of Dr Arnold's volumes, no history, (except Niebuhr's, whose style is often obscure) of this wonderful people existed, commensurate either to their dignity, their importance, or their intimate connection with modern institutions. In the preparation and composition of the history, Dr. Arnold expended many long years, and bent to it the whole force of his great energies. It is a work to which the whole culture of the man, from boyhood, contributed—most carefully and deeply meditated, pursued with all the ardor of a labor of love, and relinquished only with life. Of the conscientious accuracy, industry, and power of mind, which the work evinces—its clearness, dignity, and vigor of composition—it would be needless to speak. It is eminently calculated to delight and instruct both the student and the miscellaneous reader."—*Boston Courier.*

III.

LECTURES ON MODERN HISTORY.

Delivered in Lent Term, 1842, with the Inaugural Lecture delivered in 1841. Edited, with a Preface and Notes, by Henry Reed, M. A., Prof. of English Literature in the University of Pa. 12mo. $1 25.

"The Lectures are *eight* in number, and furnish the best possible introduction to a philosophical study of modern history. Prof. Reed has added greatly to the worth and interest of the volume, by appending to each lecture such extracts from Dr. Arnold's other writings as would more fully illustrate its prominent points. The notes and appendix which he has thus furnished are exceedingly valuable."—*Courier and Enquirer.*

IV.

RUGBY SCHOOL SERMONS.

Sermons preached in the Chapel of Rugby School, with an Address before Confirmation. One volume, 16mo. 50 cts.

"There are thirty Sermons in this neat little volume, which we cordially recommend to parents and others, for the use of the young, as a guide and incentive to deep earnestness in matters of religious belief and conduct; as a book which will interest all by its sincerity, and especially those who have become acquainted with Dr. A. through his Life and Letters, recently published by the Appletons."—*Evening Post.*

V.

MISCELLANEOUS WORKS.

With nine additional Essays, not included in the English collection. One volume, 8vo. $2 00.

"This volume includes disquisitions on the 'Church and State,' in its existing British combinations—on Scriptural and Secular History—and on Education, with various other subjects of Political Economy. It will be a suitable counterpart to the 'Life and Correspondence of Dr. Arnold,' and scholars who have been so deeply interested in that impressive biography will be gratified to ascertain the deliberate judgment of the Author, upon the numerous important themes which his 'Miscellaneous Works' so richly and clearly announce."

VI.

THE LIFE AND CORRESPONDENCE OF THOMAS ARNOLD, D. D.

By Arthur P. Stanley, A. M. 2d American from the fifth London edition. One handsome 8vo. volume. $2 00.

"This work should be in the hands of every one who lives and thinks for his race and for his religion: not so much as a guide for action, as affording a stimulant to intellectual and moral reflection.' —*Prot. Churchman.*

www.ingramcontent.com/pod-product-compliance
Lightning Source LLC
LaVergne TN
LVHW021402110826
845150LV00007B/1749

* 9 7 8 1 4 2 5 5 1 3 4 0 5 *